The Tale of the Old Fisherman

CONTEMPORARY URDU SHORT STORIES

The Tale of the Old Fisherman

CONTEMPORARY URDU SHORT STORIES

Edited and with an Introduction by
Muhammad Umar Memon

University of Wisconsin-Madison

An Original by Three Continents Press

First Edition by
    Three Continents Press, Inc.
    1901 Pennsylvania Avenue, N.W.
    Washington, D.C. 20006

Library of Congress Cataloging-in-Publication Data

The Tale of the old fisherman : contemporary Urdu short stories / edited and with an introduction by Muhammad Umar Memon. – 1st ed.
        p.   cm.
    Translation of Urdu stories.
    "An Original by Three Continents Press."
    Contents: Purvai–the easterly wind / Zamiruddin Ahmad – The wagon / Khalida Asghar – Of coconuts and chilled beer bottles / Masud Ashar – Fire, ashes, and water / Saleem Asmi - The seventh door / Intizar Husain – The tale of the old fisherman / Abdullah Hussein – Two men, slightly wet / Iqbal Majeed – The poor dears / Hasan Manzar – The dark alley / Muhammad Umar Memon – Wood chopped in the jungle / Surender Parkash – Siberia / Muhammad Salimur Rahman – Scorpion, cave, pattern / Enver Sajjad.
    ISBN 0-89410-681-3 (cloth) : $25.00. – ISBN 0-89410-682-1 (pbk.) : $11.00
    1. Short stories, Urdu–Translations into English.   I. Memon, Muhammad Umar, 1939-
PK2190.T27   1991
891'.43930108–dc20

91-50117
CIP

Excerpts from MYSELF WITH OTHERS by Carlos Fuentes. Copyright © 1981, 1983, 1986, 1988 by Carlos Fuentes. Reprinted by permission of Farrar, Straus & Giroux, Inc.

Acknowledgments

All translations except "The Tale of the Old Fisherman," were especially commissioned for this volume, which was conceived a good decade ago. The inordinate delay in putting the work together, for which the editor assumes full responsibility, and the uncertainty about its publication led some of the translators to seek other channels of publication. A few translations have therefore already appeared elsewhere and are reprinted with permission. The editor wishes to thank: *Indian Literature,* for "The Wagon"; *Edebiyāt,* for "Two Men, Slightly Wet"; *Urdu Canada,* for "The Poor Dears" and "The Dark Alley"; and Alamgir Hashmi, ed., *The Worlds of Muslim Imagination,* for "Siberia." Thanks are also due to the editors of *Mahfil* (now *Journal of South Asian Literature*) for permission to reproduce "The Tale of the Old Fisherman."

No undertaking of this sort is ever an individual effort, and this volume is no exception. I am grateful that Faruq Hassan, Wayne R. Husted, Sagaree S. Korom, Ursula K. LeGuin, C.M. Naim, Frances W. Pritchett, and Javaid Qazi graciously accepted to contribute their time and effort to make this volume possible.

Sources

"Purvai—The Easterly Wind" by Zamiruddin Ahmad: "Purvā'ī," *Nayā Daur,* Nos. 81-82, 1987 (?).

"The Wagon" by Khalida Asghar: "Savārī," *Pahčān,* Karachi: Khālid Publications, 1981.

"Of Coconuts and Chilled Beer Bottles" by Masud Ashar: "Ḍāb aur bī'r kī thanḍī bōtal," *Āṅkhōṅ par dōnōṅ hāth,* Multan: Khallāqīn, 1974.

"Fire, Ashes and Water" by Saleem Asmi: "Āg, khāk, pānī," *Sāt Rang,* Vol. 2, Nos. 11-12, 1961.

"The Seventh Door" by Intizar Husain: "Sātvāṅ dar," *Kaṅkarī,* Lahore: Maktaba-ye Jadīd, 1955.

"The Tale of the Old Fisherman" by Abdullah Hussein: "Jilyānwālā bāgh," *Savērā,* No. 31 (n.d.).

"Two Men, Slightly Wet" by Iqbal Majeed: "Do bhīgē hū'ē lōg," *Do bhīgē hū'ē lōg,* Lucknow: Nuṣrat Publishers, 1970 or 1971.

"The Poor Dear" by Hasan Manzar: "Bečārē," *Nadīdī,* Hyderabad: Āgahī Publications, 1982.

"The Dark Alley" by Muhammad Umar Memon: "Tārīk galī," *Nayā Daur,* Nos. 29-30, 1963.

"Wood Chopped in the Jungle" by Surender Parkash: "Jaṅgal sē kāṭī hū'ī lakṛiyāṅ," *Bāz-gō'ī* Delhi: Educational Publishing House, 1988.

"Siberia" by Muhammad Salimur Rahman: "Sā'bēriyā," in *Mihrāb,* ed. Ahmad Mushtaq and Suhail Ahmad, Lahore: Qausēn, 1979.

"Scorpion, Cave, Pattern" by Enver Sajjad: "Bičchū, ghar, naqsh," *Isti'ārē,* Lahore: Iẓhār Sons, 1970

To loves young and old—

Urdu, fiction, Nakako, African Violets, and a very special friend

Contents

. . . We must never find the exact identification of word and thing; a mystery, a divorce, a dissonance must remain; then a poem will be written to close the gap, but never achieve the union. A story will be told.

— Carlos Fuentes, *Myself with Others*

•

Introduction

I

Muslims arrived in India as early as 711 as part of the expedition led by the teenage Arab general Muhammad bin Qasim. Shortly thereafter, Sindh and the lower Punjab were incorporated into the Arab Umaiyad Caliphate as its easternmost outpost. The main Muslim presence in the Indian subcontinent, however, didn't begin until the early eleventh century. In 1001, from his native Ghazna—in modern Afghanistan—the Turkish Sultan Mahmud crossed over into northwest India via the Khyber Pass. Over the next quarter of a century, Mahmud launched a series of similar raids which led, eventually, to the inauguration of Muslim rule in India. This rule, through half a dozen dynasties of Turkish origin, but of unmistakable Persian culture, endured until the mid-nineteenth century, when it was replaced by the British Raj.

Urdu must have originated shortly after Mahmud's incursions into the area which now comprises roughly north-central Pakistan. The incoming Muslims constituted a small minority of foreigners, who differed from the large native population in all major respects: ethnicity, religion, culture, and language. They could carry on among themselves in their native Turkish and use Persian for administrative work, but any communication with the subject population required the development of a new lingua franca. It is likely that Urdu evolved in the wake of Ghaznavid invasions as a hybrid of some form of Old Punjabi, spoken in and around Lahore, and Persian. Later in the twelfth century, with the expansion of Muslim rule into Delhi, Urdu also absorbed some elements from the "Upstanding Speech" (*kharī bōlī*), a dialect of Old Hindi spoken in the area of Delhi.

The designation of the new lingua franca as Urdu—a word derived from the old Turkish "Ordu" meaning a "military camp" and cognate with the modern English "horde"—is of fairly late origin. It came into vogue only toward the later part of the Mughal period and stood for the language spoken by the imperial army in the military camp, which itself was designated as *Urdū-e mu'allā* (the exalted camp). Earlier, it was given different names, such as *Hindavī* or *Hindī* ("Indian"), *Dehlavī* ("of Delhi"), and later—in eighteenth century when it became a literary language as well—*rēkhta* ("mixed"). The British, however, preferred to call it *Hindustānī*.

In its grammatical structure Urdu is a member of the Indo-European family. A significant percentage of its vocabulary, mostly nouns and adjectives, however, is made up of loanwords from Persian, Arabic, and Turkish. It uses a modified form of the Perso-Arabic script as well. At the simple speech level it is more or less identical with its close kin Hindi and, as such, can easily claim about 200 million speakers in India, Pakistan, and those parts of the U.K., U.S.A., and Canada with sizeable South Asian emigrant populations. But at formal and refined speech levels, as well as in literature, the differences between Urdu and Hindi became quite stark. Today it is the official language of a multi-ethnic and multi-linguistic Pakistan and one of the fourteen "regional languages" recognized in the constitution of the Republic of India.

Urdu, or rather pre-Urdu, had evolved in response to the practical need of communication. Its main speakers were either Indian converts to Islam or émigré Muslims who had intermarried in India and made it their home. But even to these people Persian remained the preferred medium of literary expression and governmental administration. Not until the middle and later part of the eighteenth century did Urdu finally come to supplant Persian in the north as the chief literary medium, although in the south it had, under the name of *Dakanī*, already given rise to a flourishing literature two centuries earlier.

The British arrived in the subcontinent in 1608 as peaceful traders. By the mid-nineteenth century, however, the traders had terminated the Mughal Empire and emerged as the foremost power on the Indian political scene. With the Mughals removed from power, the British replaced Persian with English as the language of administration and education. Sheer political necessity (or political good sense, at any rate) led them to assign greater value to Indian "vernaculars." To Urdu among them, which had lost none of its resilience as the subcontinent's dominant lingua franca, they accorded a role just below English. The College of Fort William, founded in 1800 in Calcutta, then capital of British India, became the channel through which Englishmen were trained in the "vernaculars."

The history of an incipient Urdu literature can be traced back to the fifteenth century, although the literature itself doesn't add up to a sizeable corpus. It couldn't have been otherwise. Urdu needed legitimacy and encouragement as a literary language. When these were granted, it didn't take long to develop a body of literature, which, surprisingly from its very inception, shows a high level of sophistication, maturity, and refinement. This might have been made possible by the incorporation of Persian literary genres and conventions into Urdu. The sensibility working upon the literary material had not changed; only the language had, and then minimally. For was not the large vocabulary of Urdu, and almost all of Urdu poetry, after all drawn from Persian? The change meant, principally, a change in the use of verbal forms.

But the history of Urdu literature is preeminently the history of Urdu poetry. To the Muslim mind imaginative literature had meant, first and foremost, poetic creation. It is for this reason that the pre-modern Urdu literature abounds in poetic composition of great brilliance but lacks similar works in prose.

The development of Urdu prose received a number of powerful impulses from a variety of sources. The British, for reasons of political expediency, became instrumental in the promotion of Urdu prose, just as a similar expediency would compel them three quarters into the nineteenth century to favor Hindi. Dr. John Gilchrist, at Fort William College, acquired the services of a group of people who spoke the finest Urdu and commissioned them to put together suitable textbook materials to meet the instructional needs of young Englishmen.

Earlier, in 1792, the semi-Westernized Delhi College had also been founded (by the Muslims, however) which used Urdu as the medium of instruction and oversaw the translation of numerous Western works on social and physical sciences into Urdu.

The increasing Muslim realization of their diminished political fortunes under the British also contributed indirectly to the growth of Urdu prose. Sir Saiyad Ahmad Khan (1817-1898) and his group, notably Maulana Altaf Husain Hali (1837-1914), felt that acceptance rather than rejection of the British ways of education promised the way out of their present political insignificance. In literary terms, this meant repudiation of the modes of thinking and writing which harked back to the past.

Hali's bid for utilitarianism, Sir Saiyad's for Western rationalism, and that of the British for consolidation of the Raj all combined to produce a curious—though in retrospect not entirely unwelcome—phenomenon: the rise of written Urdu prose in a simple, direct, and unadorned style which both Sir Saiyad and Hali had taken great pains to cultivate.

II

Fiction as we know it in the West is a recent and entirely derivative phenomenon in Urdu. Its emergence was facilitated by the inexorable movement of a medieval culture—with poetry as its finest and most visible achievement—into the age of prose to meet the challenge of a Europe recently rejuvenated by the Industrial Revolution. Before this, Muslim imagination had appropriated poetry for creative expression, and at that selected largely the *ghazal* as the preeminent form to articulate and deliver its genius. Among the languages used by Muslims in the pre-modern period, Persian alone had offered a somewhat more extensive tradition of narrative fiction. Although it was available in the prose form of *dāstān*, practically all major narrative fiction was written in the verse form of *maṣnavī*. Nizami composed his epical works, especially the *Haft paykar* (Seven Portraits), in that form, as did Rumi his mystical odyssey of the soul—*Maṣnavī-ye maʿnavī*. The *dāstāns*, on the other hand, were generally not accorded the stratus of high literature; as a form they remained, according to Jiří Cejpek, midway "between epics, narrative literature and folk-tales."[1]

Urdu, whose major literary conventions and forms are borrowed from Persian, adopted the *maṣnavī* and, later, the *dāstān*, which it then relegated to the realm of folk-culture. Considerably padded with indigenous Indian elements, the Urdu *dāstān* was recited for the entertainment of the nobility and the masses, who enjoyed it for its exuberant fantasy and the use of supernatural incident and causality, but above all for its rhythmical and often rhyming prose. Quite popular as oral literature, the Urdu *dāstān* didn't even begin to take its final shape until the second half of the eighteenth century and had to wait another hundred years to be collected and printed.

Urdu fiction may begin, chronologically, from the textbooks produced under the auspices of the Fort William College, Mir Amman's *Bāgh-o-bahār* (Garden and Spring; 1801) being the most famous among them. But this fiction is not in the strict Western sense of the formal short story and novel. Neither Amman's work, nor Rajab Ali Beg Surur's *Fasāna-ye 'ajā'ib* (Tale of Wonders; 1834), written independently of the College's patronage, departs significantly from the old tradition of the *dāstān*, except perhaps in length.

The style of the *dāstān* still permeates Ratan Nath Sarshar's *Fasāna-ye āzād* (Tale of Azad; serialized between 1878-79 in the newspaper *Avadh akhbār*, where Sarshar served as editor). This despite the author's claim to offering something entirely new in Urdu. But if the *Fasāna* fails to effect a clean break from the *dāstān*, it nonetheless differs from it in important ways: the setting is contemporary, the content is in some respects new, and there is absolutely no dependence on supernatural incident.[2] More importantly, the consciousness working on the material shows a subtle acceptance of contemporary issues. Whatever else it may be, it certainly is not a novel. Its various episodes were written more by the need to fill the newspaper's columns, than by an inexorable novelistic plan or strategy.

With Deputy Nazir Ahmad (1831-1912), an older contemporary of Sarshar, the prolonged hold of the *dāstān* would finally appear to relax, only to tighten again briefly in the works of Abdul Halim Sharar, a younger contemporary of Nazir Ahmad and Sarshar.

Nazir Ahmad, who never thought of himself as a novelist, nonetheless recognized in fiction a possibility for moral education, sorely needed now that his own children were growing up and Muslim curricula tragically lacked suitable materials for the education of children and young adults. The situation was especially bad in the case of young Muslim women. Nazir Ahmad rose to fill the gap. After *Mir'āt al-'arūs* (The Bride's Mirror), he wrote several other novels,

10

the more famous among them being *Taubat an-Naṣūḥ* (Nasuh's Re-
pentance) and *Ibn al-vaqt* (The Opportunist). These works, although untainted by the *dastān*-esque ambience which haunted the
balance of prose narratives of the nineteenth century, are at any
rate compromised by their thinly veiled didacticism. The need to
moralize, which never leaves the author, discourages him from
shaping psychologically credible characters with a sense of individu-
ality, uniqueness, volition, and selfhood. Their purpose is to illus-
trate a moral point, to send a reformist message. What makes these
works readable, however, and saves them from the tedium of a
genre so pervasive in the nineteenth century is the author's uncom-
monly keen observation of contemporary reality expressed in a
crisp, vibrant style.

However, with Abdul Halim Sharar (1860-1926), a journalist and
the pioneer of the genre of historical romance in Urdu, the gains
made by Nazir Ahmad, mainly in the area of realism, would seem to
backslide into the fantasy of the *dastān*-esque. All the more remarkable in an author who was the first one to apply the term "novel" to
his works. But Sharar, who modeled himself after Walter Scott,
wrote, as Sadiq has aptly noted, less out of a feeling of romantic love
for the past than by the desire to rehabilitate Islam, by depicting "its
glories and spirit to fire the minds of his co-religionists."[3] It is perhaps the inherent therapeutic potential of these romances that ex-
plains their instant success and popularity. They were written at a
time when Muslims were on the retreat in practically all areas of
their corporate life, and their pride had been badly hurt in the 1857
war of independence, which they had lost. And although Sharar's
many romances flout with impunity every law of probability and play
fast and loose with history, they were greatly loved for their sooth-
ing effect.

III

Against this rather unremarkable background of prose narrative,
there appears around the turn of the century (in 1899, to be precise) *Umrā'ō Jān Adà* (the name of a fictitious courtesan of
Lucknow), the first true novel of Urdu. It can also be considered a
modern novel, more in the sense of fundamentals than in refine-

ments. But it is also a novel which literally springs to life without parent or precursor. Or so it would seem. There were no earlier models to follow, nor was there a tradition of narrative prose fiction, matured and refined over time, to draw on.

For its time, then, *Umrā'ō Jān Adā* is an astonishingly sophisticated piece of prose fiction. It delights and intrigues. But it can also be stuffy and cumbersome—both in the sheer magnitude of its culture-specific detail, and its occasional moralizings, which intrude on the narrative flow and tire the reader. It delights because the attitude of its author, Mizra Muhammad Hadi Rusva (1858-1931), towards his heroine, nowhere lacking in affection and warmth, is nonetheless free of sentimentality. He has sculpted her with rare sensitivity to the radical autonomy of her nature. The work's fictional space hums with her presence; her beguiling civility and charm, her resilience, but above all, her freedom from regret or self-pity over life's misfortune invest her with distinct selfhood.

Yet it is not just plausible characterization that makes *Umrā'ō Jān Adā* a unique work of novelistic art. Rusva also displays a fairly advanced understanding of the elements required for good fiction writing. He tells his story skillfully; he gives it a well constructed and coherent plot which develops according to established causality. And he also knows how to enliven the story with a subtle and witty dialogue.

Umrā'ō Jān Adā, however, remains a singular achievement. None of the works produced in the first four decades of the twentieth century, including Rusva's own half a dozen novels, comes anywhere close to the excellence of *Umrā'ō Jān Adā*.

This rather lengthy account of the Urdu novel in a work devoted to the origins and development of the Urdu short story might appear gratuitous. But is is necessitated on three counts: (1) there is scarcely anything even remotely resembling the short story in Urdu before the 1900s; (2) as forms of fiction, both share identical creative and expressive concerns; and (3) fiction in the Western sense—namely, an expressive mode which seeks to *reveal* rather than to prove or disprove some truth or insight about life by arousing, through character, incident, or both, our interest in that truth or insight at a human level—was incorporated into Urdu. Beyond that, it is not intended to imply that the borders between the two genres are nonexistent or blurred. Certainly, the two cannot be exhaustively defined by a single poetics.

IV

The didactic element, dominant in Nazir Ahmad and somewhat muted in Rusva, reappears in the three decades following *Umrā'ō Jān Adā*—a period dominated by Munshi Premchand (1880-1936). The father of the Urdu short story, he also wrote a number of novels, some quite successful, among them his last *Gaudān* (The Offering of a Cow; 1936). Just as purely instructional needs had driven Nazir Ahmad to "purposeful" fiction, so did the social and political conditions of the time propel Premchand inexorably towards defining literature as an instrument of protest, reform, and redress.

Premchand was born in India hurting from the pain of foreign domination. The country had been held hostage to the British greed for power and economic exploitation, guaranteed under the protective umbrella of the Raj and backed by its awesome military might. The slightest expression of patriotism on the part of the disenfranchised population was rewarded with unduly harsh punishments. Premchand's own first collection of patriotic tales, *Sōz-e vaṭan* (Burning Love for the Country; 1907), which he wrote under the pseudonym of Nawab Rai, was not only confiscated and publicly burnt by the British authorities for its alleged "seditious" content, but the author himself was forced into a humiliating apology. The partition of Bengal in 1905 and the indiscriminate murder of the Indians at the direct orders of General Dyer in the 1919 Jallianwala Bagh incident were not the kind of acts which a man of Premchand's patriotism and sensitivity could have easily accepted.

But Premchand's India was also hurting from its own decadence, graphically brought home to the author in the rapacity of the rich and the religious dogmatism of the upper-caste Hindus. The moneyed classes cleaned out the poor, and the higher-caste Hindu had no other words for the victim than resignation to fate as the bounden religious duty. Premchand, himself born and brought up in a village, had experienced firsthand the chilling effects of religious dogmatism and economic exploitation on the Indian peasantry. They cut deeply into his soul. The domestic and financial tensions in his own life further added to his sense of unhappiness and drove him to seek redress of all ills through some kind of action.

Politically, Premchand joined the "Non-cooperation Movement" of M.K. Ghandi and resigned his government job as Sub-deputy Inspector of Schools. In other spheres he sought reform through literature. He wrote gripping stories of the plight of the Indian peasant, victimized by perverse social and religious customs and groaning under an excessively oppressive agrarian system. Largely realistic in its depiction of rural life, the bulk of his fiction offers, curiously enough, only utopian solutions to the problems besetting the disinherited classes. And when he turns from village to urban life, his pen falters. This is only logical. He knew rural India and its conflicts more intimately than the follies and foibles of the urban classes. His characters, although painted more realistically than those of Nazir Ahmad, share the latter's flatness. Generally they remain types. Only rarely—mostly in some of his later fiction, such as the short story "Kafan" (The Shroud), do they seem to rebel against his authorial tyranny to assume some semblance of individual nature and traits.

Such criticism, however, unfairly assumes that Premchand fell short of an established fictional norm that requires unconditional regard for the autonomy of literature. In fact Premchand was more of a pioneer than the telos of a fictional expectation matured over time. The notion of literature as an autonomous domain had not yet informed the creative consciousness or the literary theory of his time. Then again, in the face of two of the most daunting enemies—foreign domination and native decadence—Premchand had little time to contemplate such niceties. Yet there is enough evidence to suggest that in his later work he was moving decisively towards some such notion of fiction.

Premchand's chief contribution lies in helping the short story emerge as a discrete narrative genre. He was also able to give it a more expansive range of topics. More importantly, he finalized as a dialectical necessity its break—long overdue—with the romantic style of writing. This style had not only dominated the bulk of the prose works of the nineteenth century but was still being vigorously cultivated by, among others, Sajjad Hyder Yaldrim and Niaz Fatehpuri. Premchand shifted the focus of fiction to contemporary social themes and brought the common man, for the first time ever, to the center stage.

In all this he was no doubt immensely aided by his extensive readings of French and Russian masters whose works had started to appear in Urdu translation at about this time. Although he liked Maupassant, he felt slightly put off by the latter's provocative treatment of sexual themes. Of the Russains Tolstoy, Chekhov, Turgenev, and Gorky, he particularly admired Gorky, in whom he found a kindred spirit. Gorky's touching portrayal of the dispossessed Russian classes, his deep concern for their well-being, and his charitable, humanistic spirit were properties which didn't fail to impress Premchand.

That he should have consciously chosen the short story at all is of some moment and consequence. Implicit in the choice is the radical belief that it no longer required the magnitude of the novel to tell a story, that the creative space provided by the short story could be pressed into the service of—indeed, help redefine—the fictional poetics of the time.

The discovery of the village and its conflicts as a potential fictional subject matter opened new possibilities for many of Premchand's contemporaries. Under his influence, Pundit Sudarshan, Ali Abbas Husaini, Akhtar Orainvi, Suhail Azimabadi, Upendar Nath Ashk, and Hayatullah Ansari wrote a number of short stories focusing on life in rural India.

V

Rusva and Premchand's legacy received an unexpected boost from the publication, in 1931, of a collection of ten short stories, *Aṅgārē* (Live Coals), by a group of four young writers comprised of Ahmed Ali (b. 1912), Sajjad Zaheer (d. 1973), Rashid Jahan (d. 1951), and Mahmuduzzafar (d. 1954)—all from the urban upper class, all highly educated.[4] The avowed aim of the work was to put literature in living contact with the socio-political reality of the time. At a deeper level, however, because the writers were very well read in Western fiction, the work introduced a more varied and relatively more complex treatment of the short story form under unmistakable Marxist, Freudian, and Joycean influences.

Thus Sajjad Zaheer, who contributed exactly half of the stories in the collection, employed interior monologue to establish a link between external reality and the psychic states of his character in the story "Nīnd nahīṅ ātī" (Insomnia; lit., "sleep does not come"). Two of his other stories, namely, "Jannat kī basharat" (Vision of Heaven) and "Dulārī" (The name of the female central character), are woven around definitive sexual themes. The former exposes the hypocrisy of the religious, the latter the sexual exploitation of the underprivileged women in urban middle-class households.

The two pieces by Ahmed Ali—who was to emerge in the 1940s as a major fiction writer, the author of the famous English novel *Twilight in Delhi*—also employ interior monologue, but in rather crude fashion. He used this device rather more successfully in some of his later fiction, such as "Maut sē pahlē" (Before Death) and "Mērā kamrā" (My Room).

Rashid Jahan's contribution commends itself to the reader more by the novelty of its themes than by its artistic execution. The most liberated woman of her time and a trained gynecologist, she was naturally concerned with the problems besetting her gender. One of her two stories in *Angārē* deals with the chilling indifference with which Indian husbands treated their wives; the other with the effects of frequent—indeed excessive—childbearing.

Mahmuduzzafar's sole contribution, "Javāṅ-mardī" (Machismo), perhaps even more simplistic than some of the other stories in the volume, is rather refreshing in the choice of its subject: the lingering male chauvinism and insensitivity even in the idealistic youth educated in the West and fired by all kinds of progressive ideals.

Although naïve and simplistic from today's perspective, these stories carried within them the germs of some of the future developments in the form. More specifically, while remaining true to the socio-political concerns of Premchand, they nevertheless expanded the thematic parameters of those concerns. For instance, gender exploitation was added to the register of reform. A corresponding expansion in the range of devices closely followed the widening of the thematic range.

Five years later these writers, along with some others, launched the Progressive Writers' Movement in Urdu, as an offshoot of the Indian Progressive Writers' Association, founded in London in 1934.[5] Under the leadership of Sajjad Zaheer, who had been drifting towards socialism during his student days in London, the Movement acquired an unmistakable Marxist orientation, which later on led a number of writers to break away from it.

The Progressive Movement sought to promote the same socially aware writing which Premchand had inaugurated in his fiction, and which Akhtar Husain Raipuri had expounded in his 1935 Urdu article "Adab aur zindagī" (Literature and Life) which bore traces of the literary assumptions of some Russian writers, among them, notably, Leo Tolstoy and Maxim Gorky. It strove, on the one hand, to expose the plight and struggle of the economically depressed classes in rural and urban settings (such as the peasantry and the proletariat) and, on the other, to articulate the political and nationalistic aspirations of a disenfranchised people seeking liberation from the Raj. The influence of the Progressive Movement was pervasive. Some writers who could not subscribe to its ideological mandate, or who found its mechanistic, formulaic view of literature both confining and insipid, still felt bound to its strident anti-imperialist stand.

While it is true that the majority of the Progressives were ideologically close to Premchand and shared his view of literature as a social chronicle, a small number of individualists among them sought to capture instead the precise color, rhythm, and smell of the evanescent world of the mind. Anything but a monolithic group, the Progressives represented, in the '30s at least, a variety of literary trends and presuppositions.

With time, however, ideological rigidity set in; the movement became doctrinaire, and started to expatiate on the essence of "progressivism" in literature. Even Sajjad Zaheer, who had earlier admitted sexual exploitation as a valid literary concern, now played it down; indeed he expunged it from the Progressive gospel as altogether reactionary. The denunciation extended even to a writer like Saadat Hasan Manto (d. 1955) who shared a number of the Progressives' socio-political concerns and many of whose themes distinctly remind one of Sajjad Zaheer's in the collection *Angārē*. Most such pronouncements were made in the journal of the Progressive establishment *Nayā adab* (New Literature), which also indulged in scathing polemics and the worst kind of innuendoes against the more independent-minded writers—the "deviationists," as the Progressives called them.

Major strides in the short story of this period were made by a few Progressive writers but mostly by those who were either outside the Progressive fold or belonged to it only nominally. Among the former, the names of Ismat Chughtai, Aziz Ahmad, Khwaja Ahmad Abbas, and Krishan Chandar stand out.

Ismat Chughtai expressed herself with unprecedented frankness about the problems besetting the middle-class Muslim woman, often aggravated—as in the story "Čauthī kā jōṛā" (approximately, The Wedding Clothes)—by gnawing poverty. Without equivocation, she dealt with the issue of female sexuality: the confusing, hesitant joy at the onset of sexual urge; the tragic repression. And in one remarkable story, "Liḥāf" (The Comforter)—incidentally, the most famous (or infamous) of her quite considerable output—she scandalized the readership by her sensitive, if somewhat crude, portrayal of lesbianism in a married woman. She is also famous for employing the exclusively female dialect of Urdu in vogue among the women of the eastern United Provinces of India. Here one might mention that the Progressive critics, such as Ali Sardar Jafri, who were only too quick to denounce Manto for his employment of sexual themes, conveniently ignored similar exploits into the forbidden realm by one of their own.

Aziz Ahmad (d. 1978), who was to emerge in the 1960s and 1970s as the foremost historian of Islamic culture in the subcontinent, was better known in the 1940s and 1950s as Urdu's leading novelist. Something of a thinker, a polyglot and a man of vast learning and refinement, he served the Progressives well: With brutal frankness and in graphic detail he portrayed the Westernized upper tiers of society as they wallowed in their unmitigated decadence, hypocrisy, eroticism, and depravity in the time just prior to the cessation of the British Raj. In his technically most competent novel *Aisī bulandī, aisī pastī* (translated by Ralph Russell as *The Shore and the Wave*), he chronicles this decay in the life of Farkhundanagar—a fictionally disguised Hyderabad, the capital of the princely Muslim state in south India, where the author grew up and was educated.

Krishan Chandar (d. 1977) and Khwaja Ahmad Abbas (d. 1987) followed the Progressive ideology to the letter in the greater part of their fiction. The former, however, has remained something of a paradox in Urdu letters. The most prolific, widely read, and popular Urdu author, Krishan Chandar's writing nonetheless reveals a fairly simple mind. No incident, national or international, and no subject under the sun was ever too daunting for him, which, in the end, and in the better part of his work, he only managed to trivialize. Take the short story "The Peshawar Express," long considered his masterwork on the theme of religious riots and murder unleashed by Partition. When the footworn and emotionally drained anthropomorphic Peshawar Express train—

having witnessed the killing of its Hindu and Sikh passengers in northern Pakistan and of the Muslim ones at the Amritsar stop in India—lumbers to a halt in Bombay, it implores in what sounds like distinctly Communist jargon that it may no longer be used to haul corpses and hate, but only relief supplies to famine-stricken areas; coal, oil and iron ore to factories; new ploughs and fertilizers to farmers; etc.—leaving the reader none the wiser about the existential situation of the characters who acted so brutally during Partition, nor indeed what this behavior signaled in wider historical and anthropological terms.

Krishan Chandar had a lyrical temperament and he wrote some of the most refined and elegant Urdu prose. He was also a deeply sensitive individual who was genuinely and passionately moved by oppression of any kind. But these attributes are rarely enough to turn fictional matter into art form. In his work characterization is often relegated to the back burner; he sensationalizes the plot, undermines causality, and eventually kills his much vaunted realism by romanticizing it. Violence, theatrics, and unabashed sentimentality are his major building blocks. They take hold of the reader with an awesome immediate force, only to leave him without substantial gains in insight after the intoxicating effect of the elegant prose has worn off.

It is perhaps understandable why Krishan Chandar, and the Progressive generally, should have taken only a limited view of contemporary man—as much a victim of socio-economic forces as in revolt against them. After all such a view was consistent with their Marxist orientation. But surprisingly, though not illogically, they also failed to recognize human anguish at any but the most superficial level. There is little awareness of the psychological effects of material deprivation in mainstream Progressive fiction, nor of the gnawing sense of alienation which must surely follow, in some individuals at least, the realization of disharmony between desire and fulfillment, real and ideal.

Alienation is a state of mind. Its treatment at the creative level must grapple with a more expansive poetics of fiction than the one employed by the Progressives—in other words, a set of narrative devices that are especially developed to give access to the consciousness of the individual, his or her mind, inner thoughts and life. Such devices would naturally place less emphasis on plot and might even replace linear order with psychic associations.

Manto, Bedi (d. 1984), and Askari (d. 1978)—writers who had broken away from the Progressives—grappled with human alienation. Which is not to say that the sources or even the flavor of alienation is identical in all three, or that it constituted their chief creative preoccupation. In fact, only Askari evinces a dominant predilection for the theme and employs it more or less consistently across his fiction. "Ḥarām-jādī" (The Bitch; lit., "the bastard woman") and "Čā'ē kī piyālī" (The Tea Cup)—written under the conscious influence of Chekhov's "The Schoolmistress" and "The Steppe," respectively—are good examples of the alienation brought on by the rupture of material harmony.

Askari appropriately entitled his collection *Jazīrē* (Islands; 1943), for each of its eight stories is like a small outcropping of land set adrift in the immense reality of the sea, moving, as it were, in its own private orbit of loneliness, never to join with others to form a single formidable land mass. They come together, only to drift farther apart. The title thus reflects the fundamental feeling of alienation shared by most of the characters. At a deeper and subtler level, the feeling is made somewhat more palpable by the choice of Christian names for the volume's many protagonists. In the ethnic and religious plurality of India, the Christians, after all, constituted—and still do—only a small, underprivileged minority—an island!

Emily, the Christian nurse/midwife in "The Bitch," feels trapped by her situation, which admits of no improvement. She goes through life accepting the inevitability of her condition, feeling pain but not reacting against it materially. The story thus presents a montage of mental events that take place in the psychic landscape of Emily. Generated, indeed, by material reality, her mental processes are not circumscribed by it. In the end, what comes through is not a replica of external reality, but an alternate reality in which the external is expanded by the mediation of a consciousness curled back upon itself in intense reflection.

In Bedi, who too was under Chekhov's influence, the feeling is so controlled and subsumed by lyricism that one might even miss it. Take, for instance, his story "Lājvantī" (the plant "touch-me-not"; its leaves fold up when touched; name of the female protagonist). Lajvanti, abducted and possibly raped by the Muslims during the religious riots of 1947, is finally reunited with her husband. Her suffering evokes only the gentlest feelings in the latter, who looks upon her as a goddess, but is unwilling to resume conjugal relations with her, out of fear that she might have been defiled. She, on her part, would rather suffer the beatings and indignities that were her fate before abduction, than be politely denied her reality as a woman. Hence a prodigious sense of emptiness and human alienation.

But alienation, understated in Bedi and gently pervasive in Askari, does not generate an anger strong enough to seek redress of situation through violent means, as it does a quarter of century later in the early fiction of Abdullah Hussein, where it assumes explosive, more often self-destructive, proportions, and is only tamed in his later, more mature work. Alienation in Manto too—where he chooses to employ it, for it is only one of his many themes—is not explosive. Still it is strong enough to produce immediate reaction in the subject. In the story "Hatak" (Insult), Saugandhi, the prostitute, having been insulted by a prospective customer, feels rejected and terribly lonely. Subsequently in what looks like a temper tantrum she throws out her lover, Madho. Feeling hemmed in by a frightening stillness, an eerie emptiness, she curls up to sleep with her mangy dog for comfort.

The partition of India in 1947 amidst the bloodshed generated by religious riots provided a ready theme for Progressive and non-Progressive writer alike. The former jumped at the opportunity to denounce it for its violence. Most of their writing on the subject tends to be rather facile and effusive, the best still coming, again, from the "independents," among them, notably, Manto, who has also given some of the finest fiction about the dispossessed, the down and out of the Indian society, the underworld characters, and about sex in its bewildering multiplicity of forms.

The Progressives had sung their swan song by the time of Partition, though they still continued, doggedly up to the mid-1950s, to exert some residual influence over the unwary and naïve younger writers. With the departure of the Raj, at least half of their ideological battle had been won. The other half, which lay in the economic regeneration of the underprivileged, soon lost its glamour to an artistically better-educated generation of writers.

The literary failure of the Progressives was perhaps inherent in their overweening commitment to society at the expense of the individual. In their repudiation of sex in any writing—unless it meant to underscore exploitation at the class or economic level, which went well with their Marxist ideology—they failed to regard it or its abuses as a moral problem. In using the issue of sex for class purposes, they employed an essentially psychological problem to create a literature of social protest, leaving untouched its great potential for exploration of human possibility. That sex within or without its culturally sanctioned forms could be enjoyable for its own sake, or that violence might also affect its perpetrator, were propositions which, though well within the artistic domain, the Progressives could have only avoided or denied as the logical necessity imposed upon them by their Marxism.

In retrospect one even doubts whether the Progressives were moved by genuine literary concerns at all. Yet, negatively, they served Urdu fiction well. By weaker and artistically less competent writing, they delineated for the more sensitive and astute what good fiction ought to be. Moreover, they accelerated the development of the Urdu short story by putting it in living contact with the realities of life. The tradition inaugurated by Premchand needed affirmation and support. The Progressives unflinchingly provided both.

To sum up: The eleven years between 1936 (marked by Premchand's death and the founding of the Progressive Movement, which he had blessed) and the partition of India in 1947 are remarkably intriguing from the perspective of Urdu literary history. The Urdu short story proper, born with Premchand, grows to maturity in that short period, in both thematic range and technical skill. The bulk of the writing of the period—which is made up of the "utilitarian" fiction of the Progressives—is, however, quite traditional in its main technical attributes. It is marked, above all, by a pronounced emphasis on linear development and sequential plot. The narrative mode is still largely "naturalistic," disinclined to turn inward, unaware—or perhaps uncertain—of the potential of devices such as the deliberate scrambling of temporality, interior monologue, and the subtle interplay of consciousness and its free associations, exemplified by James Joyce and his French forerunner, the Symbolist Édouard Dujardin. While incipient stream of consciousness and flashback can be detected even as far bask as *Aṅgārē*, a more skillful, though by no means widespread, treatment of these devices, as well as surrealism, is found in some of the short stories of Ahmed Ali, Saadat Hasan Manto, Muhammad Hasan Askari, and Qurratulain Hyder.

VI

The short story must have for its basis either social reality, the character's psychology, or both. Whichever basic block is used, the success depends on the writer's ability to leave character and incident untrammeled by his own prejudices.[6] This can be achieved either by suppressing the writer's point of view or by cancelling the narrator altogether. Although traces of authorial point of view can be found rather easily in Premchand's "The Shroud," somehow they do not intrude upon the characters and events of the story to make a difference. Two decades later, in Manto's "Phundne" (Tassels), on the other hand, the narrator is wholly suspended.

The next logical step was to develop further the expressive possibilities inherent in "The Shroud" and "Tassels" and a few other short stories by Askari and Ahmed Ali. This step was taken by what is called *jadīd afsāna* (the new or modern short story) in Urdu.

No precise date can be given for the emergence of the new short story. Periodization in literary history is a hazardous affair. While some of its rudiments can be detected as early as the 1930s, the new short story as a more widespread genre dates only from the 1960s. The names Intizar Husain, Enver Sajjad, Surender Parkash, and Balraj Manra are generally associated with the modernist phase of the Urdu short story; however, it was Manra who actually started out with a recognizably "modernist" fiction, while the other three joined him only after a prolonged apprenticeship in the traditional form.

What, precisely, does "modern" mean? In a word, "post-realism." It was increasingly apparent to the modern generation that reality was not just external but also internal, and human nature more complex than was assumed by Progressive writing. Thus, realistic and mimetic paradigms hitherto in vogue were insufficiently equipped to describe the complete reality of man. A more malleable and inclusive paradigm was in order. Dominant in such a paradigm would be the impulse to move away from "the aims, attitudes, and techniques of realism,"[7] to revise freely old notions of linearity, plot, and character, but to allow the incident to remain intact.

In Dujardin's novel, *Les lauriers sont coupés* (1887)—conceived most likely as the Symbolist revolt against the rampant naturalism of the late nineteenth century—Western fiction finally discovered the narrative means to probe into the most subliminal levels of the individual psyche, or—better yet—to let the consciousness narrate itself. The very first sentence lands the reader, directly and ineluctably, in the mind of Daniel Prince, the novel's dandy protagonist.

If Dujardin was unknown to the Urdu world, James Joyce was not. Some of the Progressives themselves were influenced by him. Interior monologue and stream of consciousness had already been employed, though somewhat tentatively as we saw, by Sajjad Zaheer, Ahmed Ali, and Askari; however, in Urdu, the use of these devices has become practically coterminus with Qurratulain Hyder. Although her literary career dates roughly from Partition, she turned toward a sustained use of stream of consciousness only with her novel *Āg kā daryā* (River of fire; 1959), which she wrote, according to Urdu critical opinion, under influences absorbed from Joyce and Virginia Woolf.

Other narrative devices, too, make their appearance at about the same time. Intizar Husain, whose literary career coincides roughly with Hyder's, experimented more or less successfully with collapsing the seriality of time and disrupting the linear sequence of events in order to articulate, on the one hand, the powerful inner tensions of his protagonist; to capture, on the the other, the precise texture of the enchanted world of his childhood.

In spite of his "modernism," Intizar Husain has been generally perceived as an excruciatingly conservative writer. This impression is partly due to the deliberately *dātsān*-esque ambiance of his stories and their continuing romance with the past. But it is a past which informs much in the present. And the mind which reflects upon it is unmistakably modern. In the short story "Ṭangēṅ" (Legs), "goat's legs" does not serve to touch up the story with a shade of the supernatural, any more than do a number of the other fantastic incidents recounted by the coachman Yasin as true, honest-to-goodness personal experiences. Rather, it serves as a powerful metaphor for the erosion of personal morality. Likewise Prince Azad Bakht meets a different end in "Kāyā-kalp" (Metamorphosis) from that reserved traditionally for the princes of popular folk-romances or *qiṣṣa*-literature.[8] Unlike a true fairy tale hero, he neither slays the white giant nor rescues the embattled princess but quietly submits to his considerably eclipsed role of anti-hero brought on by a steadily declining perception of his humanness. Turned into a fly each evening at the first rumblings of the giant's returning footfalls, and back into human form by a felicitous touch from the princess after the departure of the giant each morning, Prince Azad Bakht is stripped of the last trace of his human identity in the vertiginous rush of metamorphoses. The eventual collapse of identity is signaled one fateful evening when the princess does not change him into a fly but nevertheless finds him changed into one of his own accord the next morning. Prince Free Fortune (that's what his name means) has freely abdicated his human attributes for those of a fly! The outer change is only a metaphor for the inner change—a change of perspective on oneself and the world.

With Surender Parkash, Balraj Manra, and Enver Sajjad fictional narrative turns further inward. In other words, the traditional notion of causality is supplanted by an abstract principle of causality. Narrative foreground is deliberately muted or flattened, and the form is taxed with the entire burden of creating meaning.

Enver Sajjad, for instance, does away with all but the most crucial particularizing detail, to penetrate, seemingly, down to the essence of experience with relentless immediacy and directness. He expresses his subject through a medium—mostly the short story—stripped down to the bare minimum. The attenuated form inevitably packs his prose to the breaking point, but gives it a brutal directness and poignancy. The narrative surface in "Scorpion, Cave, Pattern"—reminiscent of Alain Robbe-Grillet—is geometric, clinically sterile, purged of all emotional toxins and sepsis. And the vision locked on the tense drama of the scorpion is—like Robbe-Grillet's on the centipede in *La Jalousie*—microscopic detached, meticulous. The shifting visual images fully engage the reader's attention and discourage any attempt to seek the meaning of the story outside of itself. Here the form is the content.

Other writers have mobilized similar modern techniques to develop a model more organically suited to the nature of experience. Their fiction subverts verisimilitude, the better to understand itself, its own processes. Hence it is self-referential or nonreferential, which makes it all the more difficult to determine the fictional subject with precision.

Indeed it is not easy to determine the fictional subject of Surender Parkash. His stories, because they do not replicate familiar reality but create a new one, are essentially experiments in what Joseph Frank has described as "spatial form." In other words, their different constituent elements (or "units") do not "unroll in time," but are "juxtaposed in space."[9] His characters often appear as pristine essences unlikely to receive palpable existence or personality—consciousnesses caught in the moment of self-communion at a pre-verbal and pre-existential level—frozen in an instant of time, as in a snapshot.[10]

"Wood Chopped in the Jungle," included in this volume, is a good illustration of his fictional design. It is made up of four discrete fragments, which alter, fuse, even intersect with one another, incrementally add or subtract the coded information, but never stray too far from the core or frame event. With proper syntax, which a reader must work out for himself or herself, they do interconnect and interlock. There is a definite but hidden geometry here. In fragment one the first-person plural narrator presents the "I," "That" city, and an empty coffin which belongs to "I" but in which "our" father's corpse is placed and "Our brother came forward and inscribed our father's date of birth and then these words: 'His body has been placed in "I"'s coffin for that day when "I" will be crucified a second time.'" In fragment three the first-person plural narrator merges with the "I", but some sense of distance between the two is still maintained by using quotation marks with the I("I"). Only in the last fragment is the "I" fully rehabilitated grammatically and semantically. And the story comes full circle when on opening the coffin washed ashore "it was my own corpse that lay in this coffin." And since that is so,

> It has been resolved that I should be crucified in the main square of the city-on-the riverbank where I live, and that my corpse be placed in this very coffin which, after it has been inscribed with my date of birth, will be dumped into the river, so that if there is need in the future, the people of that time can crucify me according to their wishes.[11]

But we still do not know the identity of the "I"? Perhaps that isn't important after all. What is important is that we as readers discover synchronic relationships among the seemingly disconnected fragments through what Frank calls "reflexive reference." Only then would the story peel off its clothes, like a stripper, perhaps, though somewhat less dramatically.

The unique incorporeality of Parkash's fiction therefore evokes shock and wonder. Unlike Premchand and most of the Progressives, the writer in his work is—to borrow a phrase from James Joyce—"refined out of existence."

The writer also disappears in some of Khalida Asghar's work. Take, for instance, the all-time favorite "Savārī" (The Wagon; lit., "a carriage, vehicle, or mount"). Telling the story in a straightforward linear manner, the first-person writer-narrator, who is swept off his feet by a disorienting attack of utterly inexplicable events, manages to retrieve the quintessential experience in its stark horror, untainted by his interpretation of its final meaning. "Couched in her language is a richly brooding anxiousness about modern man's encounter with uncontrollable forces," writes Anwar Azeem of "The Wagon."

> These forces are overwhelming. They are also terrifyingly . . . incomprehensible. . . . [Here] her concern is finally with the destiny of man, enmeshed in a labyrinth of evil forces. What does the oppressive stench which is, somehow, mysteriously connected with the wagon connote? What is the horrible, maddening, fatal truth about the strange symbol? Is not this the death-stench of carcasses? And why are the dead bodies systematically hauled away at dusk to poison the lives of men? Can the steadily intensifying and palpably evil, red glow in the sky provide a clue? Is this then the horrible, uric, rationally inexplicable, stinking monster of violence and war? The response to it of the story's sensitive characters guides our own. The evil of the wagon is pervasively obnoxious and revolting no doubt. But its disbolic power derives precisely from the fact that its origins are swathed in the darkness. Khalida Ashgar's art aims at focusing the light of awareness upon the specific nature of evil. Yet she refrains from offering a cut and dried solution. Nor does she articulate evil's nature definitively. She is only concerned with evoking the full sense of the horror of evil, and to suggest tacitly that such awareness must lead to its annihilation.[12]

Azeem has no doubt read his own meaning into "The Wagon," just as Ismat Chughtai did hers when she thought that it was inspired by the carnage resulting from Pakistan's military action in 1971 in what is now Bangladesh. The story, however, easily predates the incident by a half decade, if not more. I do not mention Chughtai facetiously. This type of fiction steers clear of temporal and spatial specificity, and thus achieves freshness, relevance, and contemporaneity in any period.

Saleem Asmi, who, regrettably, has written very little, stands out for his remarkable grasp and innovation in the use of narrative technique. In "Fire, Ashes and Water," the only successful story of its kind, he has employed multiple-narrators to view an extremely complex event from three separate perspectives. The atmosphere is haunting, full of brooding melancholy and prescience. And one walks away from the terrible feeling of a lush meadow laid to waste in the wake of a terrible storm whipped up by the violence raging deep within the human psyche.

These stories can scarcely offer an apprehension of reality, though they do invite the reader to reflect and feel with the writer what must inevitably remain quite elusive—the experience not in retrospect or vanquished—vanquished, that is, by a mediating point of view—but unfolding, out there, before the eye in its pristine, unreferenced uniqueness. More importantly, being experiments in "spatial form," they undermine with varying degrees of intensity "the inherent consecutiveness of language" and thus "place a greater burden on the reader's synthesizing power than do more conventional temporal narratives."[13]

VII

Yet the modernist work and the emergent poetics have not supplanted the traditional form and its architectural coordinates. Not only is the latter alive but has even accepted subtle influences from the former. Many major and minor writers in Pakistan and India are still using it; however, time and space have permitted us to sample only a few of them here. While the modernist product has become the exclusive benchmark of some writers (Parkash, Sajjad), in others it exists in symbiotic relationship to the older form. Thus Salimur Rahman and Abdullah Hussein, who generally write in the naturalistic mode, have also used modernist devices; on the other hand, the greater part of Intizar Husain's fiction, and certainly the story selected for this volume, is still largely naturalistic.

Alienation which emerged as fictional subject with Askari, Bedi, and Manto was prompted by the material conditions of the individual. It did not follow from a cognitive exploration into the nature of *being*. In the early '60s, Balraj Manra wrote stories about individuals—as, for example, the group of well-to-do, mobile, and highly successful young men in "Khudkushī" (Suicide)—who felt estranged from their environment largely because of their perception of life's essential boredom and absurdity. His fiction on the theme of alienation and ennui, although entirely derivative of French existentialism, nonetheless posits the problem in indigenous terms. In Abdullah Hussein, on the other hand, alienation became the unavoidable twin of knowledge. It invariably drove its victim to feelings of guilt and exile, and, eventually, to self-destruction. Most of his stories probe with both masterful precision and exquisite balance the condition of modern man at odds with himself.

But in the piece sampled here—an extract from his early novel *Udās naslēn* (Sad Generations)—Hussein is concerned with the effects of the Raj on modern subcontinental history. Drawing on the 1919 massacre of Indians by the British at Jallianwala Bagh neighborhood of Amritsar, "The Tale of the Old Fisherman" weaves the personal, historical, and social texture of a society into a fascinating story. In its controlled emotion the piece, moreover, provides a refreshing counterpoint to Krishan Chandar's two rather gushy stories about the same incident, viz.: "Amritsar before Independence" and "Amritsar after Independence."

Zamiruddin Ahmad (d. 1990), Hasan Manzar, Salimur Rahman, and Iqbal Majeed share with Hussein his preference for a more straightforward narrative style. In "Sā'bēriyā" (Siberia), for instance, Rahman keeps the structure quite simple, but invests the narrative with unusual profundity by creating the illusion of snow in a city far removed from the path even of the most ambitious snowflake. This anomaly becomes the point from which an ancient fear radiates out and generates in the reader its own myriad epiphanies of horror. No attempt is made to fix the meaning, but the atmosphere, like a powerful spell, keeps the reader locked in a vague feeling of anxiety and troubled anticipation. Incidentally, if it is any clue, "Siberia" was written during the totalitarian regime of the late President Zia-ul-Haq.

The searing conflicts generated by regional and religious chauvinism in a highly exploitative society, or even by one's own unarticulated dark psychological promptings, is the source from which Hasan Manzar draws the subject matter of his stories. Among contemporary Pakistani writers, he stands out for experimentation with the widest possible range of subjects and for diversity of locale. In "The Poor Dears," the situation of an economically impoverished contemporary Pakistani family is seen from the perspective of an expatriate South Asian writer living in London. In all their banality and hypocrisy, the widowed lady and her two daughters inspire in the reader only the gentlest feelings of regard and understanding. And one walks away feeling strangely nourished by a secret knowledge: wisdom is compassion.

Iqbal Majeed has also written on a variety of subjects. In his celebrated story "Pēṭ kā kēṅčvā" (The Tapeworm), he exposes, with precision and economy, the ongoing conflict between the rational self and inherited religious values. The protagonist, who finds religious rites of any kind at odds with his unbending rationalism, is caught in a strange predicament: the dead body of his four-year-old boy is awaiting disposal and he must decide on the final rites, as none accepted by tradition and society would be acceptable to him. The heart-tearing conflict is acted out in the form of a brutal dialogue between him and his alter ego, which he identifies as the parasite within his belly. The focus of Iqbal Majeed's more recent fiction—written in the form of a series entitled "The Jungles are being Chopped Down," where each piece is both complete in itself and interconnected thematically with the others—is the specific political and cultural problems besetting Muslims in contemporary India. In "Two Men, Slight Wet," the creative vision is trained on a delightfully subtle point, which any effort to explicate would only ruin.

Zamiruddin Ahmed's forté is understatement and evocation of senses. In a simple, austere idiom, he weaves narratives of exceptional depth and beauty. Duplicity in interpersonal relationships and the suppressed sexuality of middle-class women—often Muslim and married—are his two major themes. In an early story, "Pahlī maut" (The First Death), he shows how the hypocrisy of an otherwise respectable and religious family subjects a tender young boy to the devastating experience of moral death, how his innate, opulent sense of "right" is inevitably smothered. But in "Purvai—the Easterly Wind," and its close kin "Sūkhē Sāvan" (Dry Rains), he has produced two of the loveliest and best-executed stories of the joyous, if controlled, celebration of the senses in recent Urdu fiction.

Intizar Husain, whose later fiction draws on morality, conscience, being, and identity for subject matter, portrays in his early work, "The Seventh Door," the tragic, if inevitable, rupture of harmony between man and nature. The pre-pubescent boy, "torn between his carnal nature and his inborn spiritual yearnings,"[14] finds his resolve giving way in the face of constant proddings by his cousin—the little girl Munni, who arouses in him the first, vague feelings of sexual attraction—to capture the pigeon that has lived in the ancestral house from as far back as he could remember. The pigeon, which serves as a symbol of spiritual perfection in Husain, however, flies away, precipitating the boy's fall from the state of grace, from primordial innocence.

In the euphoria attending the birth of Pakistan on 14 August 1947, few individuals bothered to reflect on the formidable problems inherent in uniting a culturally plural society. Or, perhaps, it was assumed that such ethnic, linguistic, and cultural diversity as existed would somehow dissolve in a view of nationhood derived from religious unity. But the eastern (Bengali) wing of the country, separated from its western counterpart by a 1000 miles of Indian territory, had almost from day one become utterly disenchanted with the country's political system. Within twenty-four years of its birth, Pakistan split up. Yet the crucial event failed to inspire a sizeable and artistically competent Urdu writing affording insight into the meaning and consequence of Pakistan's national disaster. In the generally simplistic, emotional, and effusive character of the surprisingly meager writing that was nevertheless produced, the stories of Intizar Husain and Masud Ashar immediately stand out for their deep humanistic concern.

Easily half the stories in Ashar's first collection, *Āṅkhoṅ par dōnoṅ hāth* (Eyes Covered With Both Hands), but especially "Of Coconuts and Chilled Beer Bottles," included here, capture with remarkable realism and tragic clarity the tense character of Bengali-West Pakistani relations, the atmosphere of deep mutual distrust in the period just prior to the breakup of the country. Even today most Pakistanis cannot believe that the Bengalis' should have gone their separate way. This story, the only one of its kind, underscores with brutal frankness the falsity of such expectations. The hurt felt by the Bangalis, the depth of their alienation comes palpably alive in this work which is both even-handed and full of empathy.

The influence of the modernists such as Surender Parkash and Enver Sajjad, which has been received by a whole generation of younger writers, still hasn't fully jelled into an enduring artistic expression. One could perhaps make an attempt to identify the source of the problem. It stems, in the main, from the conflict between plot and character. While they have given up the latter—or, if that is too radical, depersonalized it—they have not worked out arresting the former, in most cases. Their fiction is distinguished by a multiplicity of incidents, but in the absence of real flesh-and-blood characters, mere incident can scarcely engage the reader at a human level or sustain his or her interest.[15]

VIII

In spite of its technical and thematic wealth, the Urdu short story remains largely unknown in the West. Few good translations are available for the enterprising and discerning reader. Those both good and accessible record its development, but only partially. They concentrate, for the most part, on the works of a few old masters such as Manto, Bedi, Ahmed Ali, Krishan Chandar, Aziz Ahmad, Ismat Chughtai, and Ahmad Nadim Qasimi, but seldom venture into the hesitant, complex world of the contemporary writer. I have therefore tried to select writers who have received little or no attention in a Western language, even if in doing so I may have picked up one or two rough-hewn and tentative pieces. The sampled writing comes entirely from the work produced since Partition. My intention has been to present the texture and flavor of the modern Urdu short story, both as a daring experiment and as a more refined heir to the traditional form. I have also done my best to keep a balance between the two types.

The dozen or so stories offered here are basically those that I have found significant and enjoyable. Choice cannot escape prejudice, and for that reason, neither can the present selection. It is also not exhaustive. Indeed it cannot be. For every writer included here there are easily five or six which I've had to leave out. But their exclusion is not motivated by the desire to belittle or ignore their contribution. My only regret is the absence of Qurratulain Hyder and Naiyer Masud from this collection. They were part of the work's plan from its inception. But for a variety of reasons, suitable translations of their writings couldn't be obtained. The regret is especially heart-wrenching in the case of Naiyer Masud. His fictional world is entirely underivative and unrivaled. In its dreamy wistfulness it is *sui generis* and, lamentably, nearly untranslatable.

Authors appear strictly according to the alphabetical order of their last names, not according to their importance or seniority in the field. The purpose is to void all judgement and share with the reader what must inevitably remain the product of one man's very personal aesthetic prejudice.

Rather than clutter up the text with explanations of the culture-specific words retained in the original Urdu, I have relegated them to a glossary at the end of the book, where they are fully transliterated. I have also tried to keep them to a minimum, explaining only those without which the text would itself remain unintelligible, and to italicize them only at first occurrence in the text. Also, rather than transliterate, I have opted in favor of giving the writers' names in their conventional South Asian spelling, but I have fully transliterated all Urdu titles and words occurring in the Introduction, Sources, Glossary and Notes on Contributors.

Carlos Fuentes, remembering Alfonso Reyes, recalls with fondness: "He taught me that culture had a smile, that the intellectual tradition of the whole world was ours by birth-right, and that Mexican literature was important because it was literature, not because it was Mexican."[16] Fuentes has summed up beautifully the reason for this volume.

Muhammad Umar Memon

14 August 1988
Madison-Wisconsin

Notes:

[1] "Iranian Folk Literature," in *History of Iranian Literature*, ed. Jan Rypka (Dordrecht: D. Reidel Publishing Company, 1968), p. 642.

[2] Cf. Ralph Russell, "The Development of the Modern Urdu Novel," in *The Novel in India*, ed. T.W. Clark (London: George Allen and Unwin, 1970), pp. 112-17.

[3] Muhammad Sadiq, *Twentieth-Century Urdu Literature* (Baroda: Padamja Publications, 1947), p. 2.

[4] My discussion of *Angārē* is based largely on Carlo Coppola, "Urdu Poetry, 1935-1970: The Progressive Episode," Diss. The University of Chicago 1975.

[5] On the birth and development of this Movement, see Coppola, *Urdu Poetry*.

[6] Cf. Shamsur Rahman Faruqi, *Afsānē kī ḥimāyat mēṅ* (In Support of the Short Story [New Dehli: Maktaba-ye Jāmi'a, 1982]), p. 150.

7 Scholes and Kellogg, talking about the twentieth-century narrative, in their *The Nature of Narrative* (New York: Oxford University Press, 1966), p. 5.

8 In spite of its title, this story was not written under the influence of Kafka's "Metamorphosis." Such metamorphoses are a stock theme in Urdu bed-time fairy-tales, *qiṣṣa*, and folk-romances.

9 Joseph Frank, "Spatial Form in Modern Literature," in his *The Widening Gyre: Crisis and Mastery in Modern Literature* (New Brunswick: Rutgers University Press, 1963), p. 10.

10 Cf. Shamsur Rahman Faruqi, preface, in Surender Parkash, *Dūsrē ādmī kā drā'ing rūm* (Another Man's Drawing Room [Allahabad: Shab-Khūn Kitābghar, 1968]), penultimate page of the preface.

11 This translation is by Sagaree S. Korom, for which see this volume.

12 "Contemporary Urdu Short Story: Myth and Reality," in *Indian Literature* 19:6 (1976), 19-20.

13 Jeffrey R. Smitten, paraphrasing Joseph Frank, in *Spatial Form in Narrative*, ed. Jeffrey R. Smitten and Ann Daghistany (Ithaca and London: Cornell University Press, 1981), pp. 17-21.

14 Javaid Qazi, "The Significance of being Human in Intizar Husain's Fictional World," *Journal of South Asian Literature* 18:2 (1983), p. 187.

15 For some of these insights I am indebted to Shamsur Rahman Faruqi.

16 In *Myself with Others* (New York: Farrar, Straus & Giroux, 1988), p. 19.

Zamiruddin Ahmad

Purvai—The Easterly Wind

ZAMIRUDDIN AHMAD

The boy lifted his head from the notebook and looked at the closed door behind which his father was changing his clothes.

"Father," he said, "what does *purva* mean?"

The answer came from the kitchen instead, where his mother was frying *parathas* for breakfast: "*Purvai.*"

"The wind that blows in an easterly direction?"

"No," she answered, lifting the paratha from the skillet and stacking it on the pile in the breadcloth, "rather, the wind that blows from the east."

"It's also called *purvayya*—isn't it?"

The door opened. The father, buttoning up the front of his shirt, walked onto the veranda where one three-legged chair and three perfectly good ones stood flanking a round table covered with a plastic cover. A schoolbag lay open on the table before the boy who sat in one of the chairs, bent over a notebook on which he was writing something.

The father buttoned his right sleeve and asked, "What's this all about?"

"Oh, I've got to make a sentence."

"So have you made one?"

The boy gently pushed the notebook toward his father. The latter looked down at it and red out loud: "If the wind blows from the east, it's called purvai." After a pause he remarked, "But that's the meaning!"

"So?" the boy scratched his head.

In walked the mother holding a plate with a paratha and a small serving of spiced scrambled eggs. She set the plate before the boy and said, "Write!"

The boy promptly bowed his head over the notebook again.

"One of the effects of purvai is that it cheers up the saddest person, for a while at least, and . . ."

The boy lifted his eyes from the notebook and fixed them on his mother's face. She thought for some time and then said, "That'll do. Get rid of the 'and'!"

The boy dutifully struck out the word.

Meanwhile she quickly returned to the kitchen adjoining the veranda with its door opening onto a small courtyard.

The boy shut the notebook, stuffed it into his schoolbag, and began hurriedly eating his breakfast. After he was done eating, he walked to the water-tank in the courtyard by the kitchen door and rinsed his mouth a few times. He dried his hands on a small towel hung on a clothesline in the courtyard, slung the schoolbag on his shoulder, and said, "Mother, I'll be late this evening. There's a field hockey match."

He then said goodbye to her, unlatched the courtyard door and scurried out.

Not long afterwards she returned with a plate: a couple of parathas and a small portion of some gravied meat dish left over from the previous evening. She put the plate before her husband, who was now ensconced in the same chair earlier occupied by the boy.

He stared at the plate. "No scrambled eggs for me?"

"There was just one egg," she answered, walking back to the kitchen. "I'll get some more in the evening, on my way home from work. Today's payday."

Back in the kitchen she sat down on the low wicker stool. She took out a piece of stale bread from the breadcloth, broke off a morsel, dipped it in the gravy left over in the pan, popped it into her mouth and started to slowly chew. After a couple of mouthfuls, she put the bread into the cloth.

"Aren't you going to eat breakfast?" he called, mopping the plate clean with the last of his bread.

"Oh, I've already eaten," she replied from the kitchen, removing the pot from the stove and pouring the boiling water into the tea kettle.

"When?"

"While you were bathing."

He heard the sound of a spoon being twirled in a cup and asked, "You'll at least make me some tea, or . . .?"

In response she promptly walked in with two cups neatly placed on saucers. She put one down before him and the other before herself, then settled into an empty chair.

He took a sip of the steaming brew and absent-mindedly began to scratch at the plastic tablecloth with his fingernail, trying to take off the stubborn stain left there by lentil gravy.

She too took a sip and said, "Never mind, I'll clean it off."

They sipped their tea for a while. After some time he said, "This is the second day in a row that I've had to wear the same shirt."

"Oh well. The laundryman never shows up on time. We'll have to find another."

"But maybe a couple of shirts could be washed at home."

"Why not?" There was a sharp sound as the teacup hit the saucer. "The whole pile of dirty laundry could be washed at home."

He was stunned. "Now you're cross with me."

She didn't bother to respond.

He gently took her hand and began to caress it. But she pulled it away—brusquely. He rose and strode toward the back of her chair and installed himself behind her, so close that only the thin wooden back of the chair separated their bodies. He put his palms on her pale cheeks, stooped over her and kissed her matted hair. Then he raised his right finger and touched her gently across her firmly closed lips. Both his hands slid down along her loose hair, lingered awhile on her shoulders and then wandered slyly further down.

She drew back and sprang to her feet. "I have a lot of things to do . . ."

He snickered—out of embarrassment.

"I've got to do the dishes, make the beds, take a bath . . ."

He grabbed her shoulders and pressed on them to force her to sit down. Then he pulled over a chair, sat down in it facing her and said, "What's the matter?"

"Nothing," she said, fixing her gaze on her unadorned nails.

"Look at me!"

But she didn't; instead, she said, "This isn't the right time."

"And last night?"

"I had a headache."

He laughed. "You're a great one for making excuses." There was a trace of sarcasm in his voice.

She collected the teacups and started off for the kitchen. Her ample buttocks, swaying beneath the folds of her sari, touched off a wave of excitement throughout his body before they dissolved into the grey darkness of the kitchen.

Just as she was stepping out of the store her eyes fell on a chauffeur-driven car parking some distance away on the opposite side of the street. A man sat in the rear, his head resting comfortably against the back of the seat. She started. The chauffeur got out, walked back and opened the rear door. She quickly slipped behind a tree next to the sidewalk. A tallish man, with a slightly dark complexion, wearing a suit and tie and a pair of shiny shoes, stepped out. After exchanging a few words with the chauffeur he walked away from the car and entered a nearby lane. The chauffeur returned to sit in the car.

Her throat constricted and went completely dry; her feet felt incredibly heavy; and she broke into a fine sweat. She felt as though her eyes were ready to pop out of their sockets and follow the man into the lane. She swallowed uneasily once or twice and nervously rubbed first her forehead and then her temples. She took the end of her sari lying over her shoulders and carefully covered her head with it and came out from behind the tree. She took a few hesitant steps toward the other side of the street, but faltered. She stood still, vacantly staring at the car for a few moments. Then she hastily crossed the street, walked up to the parked car, and stopped a couple of feet away from the chauffeur, unable to make up her mind whether she wanted to stop or move on ahead.

The chauffeur examined her from head to toe. Her grip on the shopping-bag tightened. She started to walk over, but then suddenly midway she did an about-face and began to walk away.

This time the chauffeur looked only at her face.

She turned around again and took a deep breath. Then she walked back to the car and asked the chauffeur, "Who was that gentleman?"

Her question had the casualness of one pedestrian asking another for the time or an address.

The chauffeur eyed her over again and replied, "He's our guest."

"Your guest?"

"Yes. I mean he's visiting my boss. He's from Pakistan."

She hesitated for a bit, then asked, "His name is Masrur Ahmad—isn't it?"

The chauffeur, who had meanwhile started to light a cigarette, blew out the match and tossed it out the window. It landed a few inches from her sandals.

"Don't know," he said. "The boss calls him Qazi-ji."

"Qazi Masrur Ahmad," she said, as if to herself. "His full name is Qazi Masrur Ahmad."

"Could be," the driver said indifferently, and through the windshield he quickly fixed his gaze on a girl in tight clothes who was walking up ahead.

A car, driven by a young woman, passed by. Another young woman sat next to the driver, her radiant hair blowing in the wind. The rear seat was occupied by a frail man and a portly woman.

She squashed the burnt match-stub with the tip of her sandal, opened the shopping bag, peered around in it, and, walking in a semi-circle around the rear of the car, came to a clothes store and stopped in front of it. After a while she walked back to the chauffeur by the same route.

"He's brought his wife along too—hasn't he?" she asked, in the manner of a child asking for something nearly impossible to get.

The chauffeur looked at her as though she was crazy. He was apparently irritated at her for coming back and pestering him with yet another question. But, being basically a courteous man, he replied gently, "Wife! No. Qazi Sahib is still a bachelor."

She quickly thanked him. She turned around, cast a sweeping look down the lane and started off toward the bus station with soft, brisk steps.

When the father, carrying a bundle of files, came into the house, he found the boy at the table doing homework. He put the bundle on the table, sat down in a chair, looked around and asked, "Where's your mother?"

"Bathing."

He heard the sound of water splashing in the bathroom.

"This time of day?"

The boy didn't answer.

The plastic tablecloth suddenly caught the man's eye. It looked spotlessly clean and shiny. The floor in the veranda too looked immaculate, still slightly wet. Perhaps it's just been mopped—he thought. The courtyard floor also looked a bit wet here and there. The house had only three rooms, each with its door opening onto the veranda. He looked at the first door, then at the second, and then at the third: each looked clean, thoroughly wiped, he speculated, with a duster. The same naked light bulb still hung directly above the table, still covered with its tenacious pile of dust, but somehow he felt it burnt much brighter today.

The sound of bathing ceased. Presently the door opened and she emerged, wearing fully starched, light green *pajama*-trousers and a *kurta*-shirt of the same color, with her wet hair wrapped up in a towel.

"It's late," she said, stopping by her husband. "I missed the six o'clock bus."

Waves of perfume wafted from her body. Her cheeks were flushed. The naked light bulb in the veranda seemed to have set off a whole array of tiny sparks in her eyes.

"Didn't you take a bath in the morning?" he asked, tearing his eyes away from the flashing pink of her cheeks.

"I couldn't. I was running late."

She proceeded toward the same door from which her husband had come out buttoning his shirt earlier in the morning.

"How about getting me a cup of tea?"

"Sure. But let me dry my hair first."

She went into the room. He yanked out a pack of cigarettes and a box of matches from his coat pocket, lit a cigarette and puffed on it.

In the meantime the boy finished his homework, picked up his school things and left for the middle room.

After the last drag the husband threw the cigarette butt down on the floor and squashed it with his shoe. Just as he was getting up, she came out of the room, her hair free of the towel and now spread loosely on her shoulders. The folds of her stiff, starched *dupatta* seemed to have frozen over her breasts. Holding the wet towel in her hand she walked to the courtyard and hung it on the clothesline.

She was about to step into the kitchen when the boy called, "Mother."

"Yes, Munna?"

"I'm hungry."

"All right."

"He hasn't eaten yet?" the father asked.

She shook her head.

"How come?"

"Oh, he had a cup of tea with a couple of pieces of toast after he got home from school. He said he wasn't feeling very hungry."

The boy came in and said, "Mother, I want supper."

"Come on Munna. Don't be so impatient. Let me fix tea for your father. Then I'll feed you."

The boy returned to his room. As she was just stepping into the kitchen, her husband got up form his chair and said, "Never mind."

"Why?"

"Let's eat supper instead. I'm hungry too."

Sounds of banging pots and pans started to pour out of the kitchen. The boy turned on the radio. The father went into the room to change, then into the bathroom.

In the meantime, she set the table and brought out the food. "All right Munna," she called out, taking the middle chair, "dinner's on."

The boy turned off the radio and came onto the veranda. His eyes fell on the platter in the middle of the table. "Wow!" he let out a joyous cry, "Pilaf today!"

The husband had just dried his hand and mouth on the wet towel hanging on the clothesline in the courtyard and was back on the veranda. "Pilaf?" he said, somewhat surprised.

She held out the platter to him and said, "I got off from work a little early today; so I thought I might cook something special." She then offered him the bowl of spicy yoghurt *raita.*

He took a generous helping of the pilaf and poured some raita on it. She served more than half of the remaining pilaf to the boy and dumped the rest on her plate, then pushed the raita toward the boy. The boy took some and set the bowl before his mother.

"Very tasty," the husband remarked after the first mouthful.

"Yeah," the boy, his mouth full, chimed in.

She smiled.

After the supper dishes were cleared away, she went into the kitchen and promptly returned with a cardboard box which she set on the table.

"My, my, what a treat!" the husband exclaimed, opening the box. "What's the occasion? Did you get a raise or something?"

He picked up a *gulab-jaman* and popped it into his mouth.

"Oh no," she said, suddenly feeling a little embarrassed. "For days now Munna has been begging for sweets. So I thought I might just as well get some. That's all."

Then, looking at the boy, she said, "Have some."

The boy picked out a *laddu*. So did the father. But she took a square of *barfi*.

Presently the boy took a gulab-jaman but, before stuffing it into his mouth, said, "Mother Siraj Sahib was telling us that the purvai also has another effect . . ."

"I know," she said, very softly.

"And what's that?" the father asked.

"When it blows, it causes old hurts to start aching again . . . Is that really true?"

"Yes," she answered, again very softly.

"Have some more," her husband offered, holding the box.

"That's enough for me," she said.

A half hour or so later she went into the kitchen, but returned right away. "What's the rush?" she said. "I can always do the dishes in the morning."

"Yes," the husband, bent over a file, said, without lifting his head.

After some time she went into the boy's room. When she returned she said, settling back in her chair, "He's fast asleep."

"Yes," he nodded, again without bothering to lift his head.

After a while she got up and brought a magazine from her room and started reading it. But when he bent down to pick up a fresh file from the floor he looked at her out of the corner of his eye and realized that she really wasn't reading the magazine at all; instead, she was looking intently into the yawning darkness of the courtyard.

When he lifted his head again to light a cigarette, he found her reading the magazine. She looked at him over the magazine, smiled sweetly, and resumed her reading.

After a bit, she slapped the magazine shut and got up. "Well, I'm going to bed."

"You go on. I'll be there in a while."

She went into her room. The sound of her humming continued for a while, then the quiet was absolute.

The moist, thick darkness oozing down from the sky had covered the length of the courtyard; the noise of the traffic outside on the street had grown progressively fainter and ultimately died down; and the bark of a solitary dog arose somewhere far away. He decided it was time to turn in. He closed the last of the files and placed it on top of the pile, rubbed his aching eyes, lit a cigarette and got up. He then turned off the veranda light, noiselessly pushed her door open and went in.

His eyes fell on their twin beds, headboards snug against the back wall. The small shaded lamp on the low sidetable lodged between the beds was still on, its dim glow barely reaching above their beds.

She was sleeping in the bed on the right; her clothes—the same pajama-kurta suit and dupatta which only a few hours ago had sent a surge of excitement through him—and her bra lay all crumpled and bunched on the easy chair to the right of her bed. So unlike her!—he wondered, a trifle surprised. Wasn't she, after all, in the habit of neatly folding her clothes and putting them carefully away in the closet every time she changed?

He edged closer to the bed and lifted the lightweight comforter pulled over her body all the way to her shoulders. He was stunned. Free of the last restraint of modesty, her sleeping body somehow seemed fully awake in anticipation of someone. He had the curious feeling that he didn't know that body, that he was looking at it for the first time ever.

He quickly stubbed out the cigarette and, every so gently, noiselessly, sat down on the edge of her bed. She shifted; and her face, turned slightly toward the easy chair, came directly under the lamp's subdued glow. Then, as he stood watching, a faint smile swept over her sealed lips.

He put one hand over the pillow cushioning her head and the other over the pillow lodged under her arm and lowered himself over her face. His parted lips stopped inches away from her closely pressed ones. Her eyelids seemed moist. This vague suspicion was confirmed when he detected a wet spot on her pillow close by her head.

He straightened up, staring tensely for a while at her face and her breasts facing him. Then, ever so gently, he raised his index finger and touched her on the lips. Her breathing altered, as did the rhythm of her heaving chest. That faint smile abruptly departed from her lips. He held his breath and waited for a few moments. After her breathing returned to normal and the heaving in her chest subsided, he got up, taking care not to make the slightest sound. For the next few moments he stared vacantly at her body as it lay there comfortably stretched out, awash in its gentle, radiant heat.

Carefully he folded her clothes—her kurta-pajama suit, her dupatta, her bra—and put them neatly on the easy chair before retiring to his bed. He sat on it for quite a while.

She turned over in bed. Her face was now turned toward him. A smile—the sign of some rich, honeyed dream—was radiating form her lips and the corners of her eyes, bringing to the fresh pink of her cheeks a more vibrant color. The other pillow was hugged tight to her bosom.

He stretched out his arm and pulled the comforter over her nakedness. Then he turned off the lamp and went to sleep.

Translated by Muhammad Umar Memon

Khalida Asghar

The Wagon

KHALIDA ASGHAR

In a rush to get back to the city, I quickly crossed the dirt road and walked onto the Ravi bridge, looking indifferently at the blazing edge of the sun steadily falling into the marsh. I had a queer feeling, as though I saw something. I spun around. There they were, three of them, leaning over the bridge's guard rails and gazing straight into the sunset. Their deathly concentration made me look at the sunset myself, but I found nothing extraordinary in the scene; so I looked back at them instead. Their faces, although not at all similar, still looked curiously alike. Their outfits suggested that they were well-to-do villagers, and their dust-coated shoes that they had trudged for miles just to watch the sun as it set over the marshes of the receding Ravi. Impervious to the traffic on the bridge, they went on staring at the marshes which were turning a dull, deep red in the sun's last glow.

I edged closer to them. The sun had gone down completely; only a dark red stripe remained on the far horizon. Suddenly the three looked at each other, lowered their heads, and silently walked away, toward the villages outside the city. For some time I stood watching their tired figures recede into the distance. Soon the night sounds coming to life in the city reminded me that it was getting late and I'd better rush home. I quickened my pace and walked on under the blue haze of the night sky, pierced here and there by the blinking lights of the city ahead.

The next evening when I reached the bridge, the sunset was a few minutes away. I suddenly recalled the three men and stopped to watch the sunset even though I knew Munna would be waiting on the front porch for sweets and Zakiya, my wife, would be ready for us to got to the movies. I couldn't budge. An inexorable force seemed to have tied me to the ground. Through almost all the previous night I'd wondered

47

what it was about the marsh and the sunset that had engrossed those strange men so entirely.

And then, just as the blazing orange disc of the sun tumbled into the marsh, I saw the three walk up the road. They were coming from villages outside the city limits. They wore identical clothes and resembled each other in their height and gait. Again they walked up to the bridge, stood at the same spot they had the previous evening and peered into the sunset with their flaming eyes filled with a dull sadness. I watched them and wondered why, despite their diverse features, they looked so much alike. One of them, who was very old, had a long, bushy snow-white beard. The second, somewhat lighter in complexion than the other, had a face that shone like gold in the orange glow of sunset. His hair hung down to his shoulders like a fringe, and he had a scar on his forehead. The third was dark and snub-nosed.

The sun sank all the way into the marsh. As on the previous day, the men glanced at each other, let their heads drop and, without exchanging a word, went their way.

That evening I felt terribly ill at ease. In a way I regretted not asking them about their utter fascination with the sunset. What could they be looking for in the sun's fading light?—I wondered. I told Zakiya about the strange threesome. She just laughed and said, "Must be peasants, on their way to the city to have a good time."

An air of strangeness surrounded these men. Zakiya, of course, could not have known it: one really had to look at them to feel the weird aura.

The next day I waited impatiently for the evening. I walked to the bridge, expecting them to show up. And they did, just as the daylight ebbed away. They leaned over the bridge and watched the sun go down, indifferent to the sound of traffic. Their absorption in the scene made it impossible to talk to them. I waited until the sun had gone down completely and the men had started to return. This would be the time to ask them what it was they expected to find in the vanishing sun and the marshes of the receding river.

When the sun had sunk all the way, the men gave one another a sad, mute look, lowered their heads and started off. But, instead of returning to the village, they took the road to the city. Their shoes were covered with dust and their feet moved on rhythmically together.

I gathered my faltering courage and asked them, "Brothers! what village do you come from?"

The man with the snub nose turned around and stared at me for a while. Then the three exchanged glances, but none of them bothered to answer my question.

"What do you see over there . . . on the bridge?" I asked. The mystery about the three men was beginning to weigh heavily upon me now. I felt as though molten lead had seeped into my legs—indeed into my whole body, and that it was only a matter of time before I'd crumble to the ground reeling from a spell of dizziness.

Again they did not answer. I shouted at them in a choking voice, "Why are you always staring at the sunset?"

No answer.

We reached the heavily congested city road. The evening sounds grew closer. It was late October, and the air felt pleasantly cool. The sweet scent of jasmine wafted in, borne by the breeze. As we passed the octroi post, the old man with snow-white hair suddenly spoke, "Didn't you see? Has nobody in the city seen . . .?"

"Seen what?"

"When the sun sets, when it goes down all the way . . .?" asked the hoary old man, rearranging his mantle over his shoulders.

"When the sun goes down all the way?" I repeated. "What about it? That happens every day!"

I said that very quickly, afraid that the slightest pause might force them back into their impenetrable silence.

"We knew that, we knew it would be that way. That's why we came. That other village, there, too . . ." He pointed toward the east and lowered his head.

"From there we come . . ." said the snub-nosed man.

"From where?" I asked, growing impatient. "Please tell me clearly."

The third man peered back at me over his shoulder. The scar on his forehead suddenly seemed deeper than before. He said, "We didn't notice, nor, I believe, did you. Perhaps nobody did. Because, as you say, the sun rises and sets every day. Why bother to look? And we didn't, when day after day, there, over there," he pointed in the direction of the east, "the sky became blood-red and so bright it blazed like fire even at nightfall. We just failed to notice . . ." He stopped abruptly, as if choking over his words. "And now this redness," he resumed after a pause, "it keeps spreading from place to place. I'd never seen such a phenomenon before. Nor my elders. Nor, I believe, did they hear their elders mention anything quite like that ever happening."

Meanwhile the darkness had deepened. All I could see of my companions were their white flowing robes; their faces became visible only when they came directly under the pale, dim light of the lampposts. I turned around to look at the stretch of sky over the distant Ravi. I was stunned: it was glowing red despite the darkness.

"You are right," I said, to hide my puzzlement, "we really did fail to notice that." Then I asked, "Where are you going?"

"To the city, of course. What would be the point of arriving there *afterwards?*"

A sudden impulse made me want to stay with them, or to take them home with me. But abruptly, they headed off on another road, and I remembered I was expected home soon. Munna would be waiting on the front porch for his daily sweets and Zakiya must be feeling irritated by my delay.

The next day I stopped at the bridge to watch the sunset. I was hoping to see those three men. the sun went down completely, but they didn't appear. I waited impatiently for them to show up. Soon, however, I was entranced by the sunset's last magical glow.

The entire sky seemed covered with a sheet soaked in blood, and it scared me that I was standing all alone underneath it. I felt an uncanny presence directly behind me. I spun around. There was nobody. All the same, I felt sure there was someone—standing behind my back, within me, or perhaps, somewhere near.

Vehicles, of all shapes and sizes, rumbled along in the light of the street-lamps. Way back in the east, a stretch of evening sky still blazed like a winding sheet of fire, radiating heat and light far into the closing darkness. I was alarmed and scurried home. Hastily I told Zakiya all I'd seen. But she laughed off the whole thing. I took her up to the balcony and showed her the red and its infernal bright glow against the dark night sky. That sobered her up a little. She thought for a while, then remarked, "We're going to have a storm any minute—I'm sure."

The next day in the office, as I worked, bent over my files, I heard Mujibullah ask Hafiz Ahmad, "Say, did you see how the sky glows at sunset these days? Even after it gets dark? Amazing, isn't it?"

All at once I felt I was standing alone and defenseless under that blood-sheet of a sky. I was frightened. Small drops of sweat formed on my forehead. As the evening edged closer, a strange restlessness took hold of me. The receding Ravi, the bridge, the night sky and the sun frightened me; I wanted to walk clear out of them. And yet, I also felt irresistibly drawn toward them.

I wanted to tell my colleagues about the three peasants who in spite of their distinctly individual faces somehow looked alike; about how they had come to the city accompanying this strange redness, had drawn my attention to it, and then dropped out of sight; and about how I'd searched in vain for them everywhere. But I couldn't. Mujibullah and Hafiz Ahmad, my office-mates, had each borrowed about twenty rupees from me some time ago, which they conveniently forgot to return, and, into the bargain, had stopped talking to me ever since.

On my way home when I entered the bridge, a strange fear made me walk briskly, look away from the sun, and try to concentrate instead on the street before me. But the blood-red evening kept coming right along. I could feel its presence everywhere. A flock of evening birds flew overhead in a "V" formation. Like the birds, I too was returning home. Home—yes, but no longer my haven against the outside world; for the flame-colored evening came pouring in from its windows, doors, even through its walls of solid masonry.

I now wandered late in the streets, looking for the three peasants. I wanted to ask them where that red came from. What was to follow? Why did they leave the last settlement? What shape was it in? But I couldn't find them anywhere. Nobody seemed to care.

A few days later I saw some men pointing up to the unusual red color of the evening. Before long, the whole city was talking about it. I hadn't told a soul except Zakiya. How they had found out about it was a puzzle to me. Those three peasants must be in the city—I concluded. They have got to be.

The red of evening had now become the talk of the town.

Chaudhri Sahib, who owns a small bookshop in Mozang Plaza, was an old acquaintance of mine. People got together at his shop for a friendly chat every evening. Often, so did I. But for some time now, since my first encounter with those mantle-wrapped oracular figures, I had been too preoccupied with my own thoughts to go there. No matter where I went, home or outside, I felt restless. At home, an inexorable urge drove me outdoors; outdoors, an equally strong urge sent me scrambling back home, where I felt comparatively safer. I became very confused about where I wanted to be. I began to feel heavy and listless.

All the same, I did go back to the bookshop once again that evening. Most of the regulars had already gathered. Chaudhri Sahib asked, "What do you think about it, fellows? Is it all due to the atomic explosions as they say? The rumor also has it that pretty soon the earth's cold regions will turn hot and the hot ones cold and the cycle of seasons will also be upset."

I wanted to tell them about my encounter with the three villagers but felt too shy to talk before so many people. Just then a pungent smell, the likes of which I'd never smelled before, wafted in from God knows where. My heart sank and a strange, sweet sort of pain stabbed my body. I felt nauseous, unable to decide whether it was a stench, a pungent aroma, or even a wave of bitter-sweet pain. I threw the newspaper down and got up to leave.

"What's the matter?" asked Chaudhri Sahib.

"I must go. God knows what sort of smell that is."

"Smell? What smell?" Chaudhri Sahib sniffed the air.

I didn't care to reply and walked away. That offensive smell, the terrifying wave of pain, followed me all the way home. It made me giddy. I thought I might fall any minute. My condition frightened Zakiya, who asked, "What's the matter—you look so pale?"

"I'm all right. God knows what that smell is." I said, wiping sweat off my brow, although it was the month of November.

Zakiya also sniffed the air, then said, "Must be coming from the house of Hakim Sahib. Heaven knows what strange herb concoctions they keep making day and night. Or else it's from burnt food. I burnt some today accidentally."

"But it seems to be everywhere ... in every street and lane ... throughout the city."

"Why, of course. The season's changed. It must be the smell of winter flowers," she said inattentively, and became absorbed in her knitting.

With great trepidation I again sniffed the air, but couldn't decide whether the sickening odor still lingered on or had subsided. Perhaps it had subsided. The thought relieved me a bit. But there was no escape from its memory, which remained fresh in my mind, like the itching that continues for some time even after the wound has healed. The very thought that it might return gave me the chills.

By next morning I'd forgotten all about that rotten, suffocating smell. In the office, I found a mountain of files waiting for me. But Mujibullah and Hafiz Ahmad went on noisily discussing some movie. I couldn't concentrate on the work and felt irritated. So I decided to take a break. I called our office boy and sent him to the cafeteria for a cup of tea. Meanwhile I pulled out a pack of cigarettes from my pocket and lit up.

Just then I felt a cracking blow on my head, as if I had fallen off a cliff and landed on my head, which fused everything before my eyes in a swirling blue and yellow streak. It took my numbed senses some time to realize that I was being assaulted once again by the same pain, the same terrible stench. It kept coming at me in waves, and it was impossible to know its source. I found myself frantically shutting every single window in the office, while both Mujibullah and Hafiz Ahmad gawked at me uncomprehendingly.

"Let the sun in! Why are you slamming the windows?" asked Hafiz Ahmad.

"The stench . . . the stench! My God, it's unbearable! Don't you smell it?"

Both of them raised their noses to their air and sniffed. Then Hafiz Ahmad remarked, "That's right. What sort of stench . . . or fragrance is that? It makes my heart sink."

Soon, many people were talking about the stink-waves which came in quick succession and then receded, only to renew their assault a little while later. At sundown they became especially unbearable.

Within a few weeks the stinking odor had become so oppressive that I often found it difficult to breathe. People's faces, usually quite lively and fresh, now looked drained and wilted. Many complained of constant palpitation and headaches. The doctors cashed in. Intellectuals hypothesized that it must be due to nuclear blasts, which were producing strange effects throughout the world, including this foul odor in our city, which attacked people's nerves and left them in a mess. People scrambled to buy tranquilizers, which sold out instantly. Not that the supply was inadequate, but a sudden frenzy to stock up and horde had seized people. Even sleeping pills fetched the price of rare diamonds.

I found both tranquilizers and sleeping pills useless. The stench cut sharper than a sword and penetrated the body like a laser. The only way to guard against it was to get used to it—I thought; and people would do well to remember that. But I was too depressed to tell them myself. Within a few weeks, however, they themselves came to live with the stench.

Just the same, the stench struck terror in the city. People were loath to admit it, but they could not have looked more tense: their faces contorted from the fear of some terrible thing happening at any moment. Nor was their fear unreasonable, as a subsequent event showed a few weeks later.

On a cold mid-December evening, I was returning home from Chaudhri Sahib's. The street was full of traffic and jostling crowds. The stores glittered with bright lights, and people went about their business as usual. Every now and then a stench-wave swept in, made me giddy, and receded. I would freeze in my stride the instant it assailed me and would start moving again as soon as it had subsided. It was the same with others. An outsider would surely have wondered why we suddenly froze, closed our eyes, stopped breathing, then took a deep breath and got started again. But that was our custom now.

That December evening I'd just walked onto the bridge when I felt as if a lance had hit me on the head. My head whirled and my legs buckled. Reeling, I clung on to a lamppost and tried to support my head with my hands. There was no lance, nor was there a hand to wield it. It was that smell—that same rotten smell—I realized with terror. In fact, it seemed that the source of the oppressive stench had suddenly moved very close to me, between my shoulder blades, near my back, immediately behind me—so close that it was impossible to think of it as apart from me.

It was then that my eyes fell on the strange carriage, rambling along in front of me. It was an oversized wagon pulled by a pair of scrawny white oxen with leather blinders over their eyes and thick ropes strung through their steaming nostrils. A wooden cage sat atop the base of the wagon, its interior hidden behind black curtains—or were they just swaying walls of darkness?

Two men, sitting outside the cage enclosure in the front of the wagon, drove the two emaciated, blindfolded animals. I couldn't make out their faces, partly because of the darkness, but partly also because they were buried in folds of cloth thrown loosely around them. Their heads drooped forward and they seemed to have dozed off, overcome by fatigue and sleep.

Behind them the interior of the curtained wagon swelled with darkness and from the heart of that darkness shot out the nauseating stench which cut sharper than a sword... Before I knew it, the wagon had creaked past me, flooding my senses with its cargo of stink. My head swirled. I jumped off the main road onto the dirt sidewalk... and vomited.

I had no idea whether the people in the city had also seen the eerie wagon. If they had, what must have they endured? I had the hardest time getting home after what I had seen. Once inside the house, I ran to my bed and threw myself on it. Zakiya kept asking me what had happened, but a blind terror sealed my lips.

A few days later a small news item appeared in the local papers. It railed against the local Municipal Office for allowing garbage carts to pass through busy streets in the evening. Not only did muck-wagons pollute the air, they also hurt the fine olfactory sense of the citizenry.

I took a whole week off from work. During those seven days, though hardly fit to go out and observe firsthand the plight of the city, I was nonetheless kept posted of developments by local newspapers. Groups of concerned citizens demanded that the municipal authorities keep the city clear of the muck-wagons or, if that was impossible, assign them routes along less busy streets.

On the seventh day I ventured out. A change was already visible. Wrecked by insomnia and exhaustion, people strained themselves to appear carefree and cheerful, but managed only to look painfully silly. Suddenly I recalled that in the morning I had myself looked no different in the mirror.

About this time, the number of entertainment programs and movies shot up as never before. People swarmed to box offices—often hours before a show—where they formed long lines and patiently waited to be let in, and then filed out from the entertainment still looking pale and ridiculous.

In the office, no matter how hard I tried, I couldn't concentrate on work. Intermittently, the image of the muck-wagon lumbering down the streets flashed across my mind. Was it really one of those municipal dump-carts? No. It couldn't be. Municipal dump-carts never looked like that eerie wagon, with its sleepy drivers, a pair of blindfolded bony oxen, black curtains and the outrageously nauseating smell. What on earth could give off such an odd smell—at once fragrant and foul!

An insane desire suddenly overwhelmed me: to rush up to the wagon, lift up those swaying curtains, and peek inside. I must discover the source of the stench!

Coming to the bridge my feet involuntarily slowed down. There was still some time before sunset and the waves of the pain-filled odor came faster and stronger. I leaned over the bridge, an unknown fear slowly rising in my throat. The bottomless swamp, its arms ominously outstretched, seemed to be dragging me down toward it. I was afraid I might jump into the swamp, sink with the sun and become buried forever in that sprawling sheet of blood.

I became aware of something approaching me—or was I myself drawing closer to something? . . . Something awaited by all men—those before and those after us. My whole body felt as though it was turning into a piece of granite, with no escape from the bridge, the miasma, the sun, for now they all seemed inseparable from my being. Helplessly, I looked around myself and almost dropped dead.

The three men were coming towards me from the direction of the countryside. As before, they were wrapped in their flowing white robes and walked with their amazingly identical gait. I kept staring at them with glassy eyes until they walked right up to me and stopped. The hoary old man was crying, and his snow-white beard was drenched in tears. The other two couldn't look up; their eyes were lowered mournfully, their teeth clenched and their faces withered by a deathly pallor.

"Where were you hiding all these days?" I said between gasps and stammers. "I searched for you everywhere. Tell me, please, what's happening to the city?"

"We were waiting. Trying to hold ourselves back. We had tied ourselves with ropes. Here, look!" They spread their arms before me and bared their shoulders and backs, revealing the deep marks of the rope.

"We did not want to come . . ." the old man said, drowned out by a fit of sobs.

"But there was no choice . . ." the second man said. Before he had finished, he doubled over. His companions also doubled over, as if unable to control a sudden surge of pain. The same wave of pain-filled stench stabbed the air about us, cutting us into halves, flooding our senses, as it scrambled past us.

"There! Look!" said the old man, pointing in the direction of the distant villages and turning deathly pale.

In the distance, I saw the wagon come up the road from behind a cloud of dust. The drowsing coachmen had wrapped their faces because of their nearness to the cutting stench.

A cold shiver ran through my spine. The eyes of the three men suddenly became dull. They were approaching their end—perhaps.

The wagon rumbled close—the stench from it draining the blood from our bodies—and then passed us. Its sinister, jet-black curtains, fluttering in the gentle breeze, appeared, oddly enough, entirely motionless.

The three men ran after the wagon, caught up to it and lifted the curtains. A spit second later, a non-human scream burst from their gaping mouths. They spun around and bolted toward the distant fields.

"What was it? What did you see?" I asked, running after them. But they did not reply and kept running madly. Their eyes had frozen in a glazed stare.

I followed them until we had left the city several miles behind us, then grabbed the old man's robe and implored, "Tell me! Please tell me!"

He turned his deathly gaze and threw open his mouth. His tongue had got stuck to his palate.

All three had become dumb.

My head whirled, and I collapsed. The three men continued to run, soon disappearing in the distance behind a spiraling cloud of dust. Slowly the dust settled and I returned home.

For months now I have searched in vain for those men. They have vanished without a trace. And the wagon . . . from that fateful evening, it too has changed its route. It no longer passes through the city. After crossing the bridge, it now descends onto the dirt trail leading to villages in the countryside.

The cityfolk are no longer bothered by the slashing stench. They have become immune to it and think it has died, like an old, forgotten tale.

But it continues to torment my body, and day and night a voice keeps telling me, "Now, your turn! Now you shall *see!*"

And this evening I find myself on the bridge, waiting for the wagon . . . waiting.

Translated by Muhammad Umar Memon

Masud Ashar

Of Coconuts and Chilled Beer Bottles

MASUD ASHAR

Separated one sings doleful songs; but when love is near—
well, there are a million things to do.

I remembered this adage when repeated requests failed to stir Husna
Begum to sing a *bhatyali*. Has the moment of togetherness arrived,
then?—I wondered. But whose union and with whom? And who must
sing a doleful song of separation: Husna Begum . . . or we?

Even though we were their guests, we couldn't have spent a more
miserable night. True, we slept indoors under mosquito nets. What of
it? The mosquitoes and other bugs got to us all the same. They kept us
awake all night long. Then there was Rahman Sahib, who babbled on
and on about all the different rivers of Bengal and about how sublime
sunsets and sunrises looked over them.

The gentleman whom Husna Begum's husband had appointed as
our guide was a certain Abul Kalam Muhammad Jaliluddin—a name
which the latter had shortened to A.K.M. Jaliluddin. (At least that is
how it appeared on his books.) During the introductions, however,
when Husna Begum's husband pronounced the "j" of Jaliluddin as a
distinct "z", we had the hardest time suppressing our laughter. Later,
aboard the cabin cruiser too, the memory of the outrageously funny
pronunciation never failed to arouse laughter. The urge was so violent
that only with the greatest difficulty did we manage to squash it. We
could neither laugh so brazenly in the presence of our hosts, nor stifle
our laughter. So we used some pretext or another to laugh, and sometimes we just pinched our noses and bent our heads. Chughtai had told

us the trick about pinching the nose. He thought it helped suppress laughter. And it also, thereby, saved us from appearing rude to our hosts. Laughter, however, took its own time to subside, but meanwhile pinching the nose made our eyes water a lot. At such times, Rahman Sahib glowered at us, full of rage, and Jalil Bhai just looked away, pretending to be busy with something or other, while we stepped out of the cabin into open air and addressed one another as "Zalil Bhai" and hurled coconut husks at flotsam in the river. In the evening, Jalil Bhai would spell out for out benefit—with statistics and all—how much we depended on the Bengalis for certain items and how we had made them depend on us for certain others. Then a raging thirst would parch our throats. While Jalil Bhai and Rahman Sahib slaked it with fresh coconut milk, Chughtai would take out some chilled beer from the bucket and pour three glasses for us. He could explain to Jalil Bhai, giving one proof after another, why coconut milk, if taken during the afternoon, constituted a real health hazard, though it was quite harm-less before sunrise or until about midday, and how "Before sunrise, coconut milk is just like beer."

But Jalil Bhai wasn't about to give in. Midway through an apparent altercation with Rahman Sahib (even when he talked normally, he appeared to be arguing), he would switch from English to Bengali. Yusuf Zai would take out a deck of cards and deftly divert us into a game of *canturi*.

At Chittagong railway terminal, a hoary old man with a long lily-white beard, suddenly planted himself in our way. He was so dark it looked as though he had come straight from shovelling coal in a locomotive.

"Going north?" he asked us abruptly in Bengali. We didn't know Bengali; so we just gawked at Rahman Sahib, hoping that he would translate the old man's words for us. Instead, Rahman Sahib gruffly told the old man to bug off. But Chughtai, now in a playful mood, answered the old man, "No, sir. We're headed south."

"*Stop slavery!*" the old man yelled in English and, securing his tattered checked loincloth on the front of his hungry, incredibly flat stomach, shoved Rahman Sahib aside and fixed his penetrating gaze on Chughtai's pink, healthy face.

But Chughtai, missing the old man's drift, snapped, "Listen Maulvi Sahib, don't try to create an impression by rattling off in your pidgin English . . ."

The old man didn't let Chughtai finish. He sprang at him and dug his bony fingers into his neck. It all happened so fast we barely had time to react. Dazed, we thought it was some kind of a joke. But it couldn't have been a joke: the old man truly had sunk his fingers into Chughtai's neck, who was choking from pressure and thrashing his hands and feet about.

Suddenly Yusuf moved forward. He grabbed the old man by the waist and with a mighty tug tore him from Chughtai and tossed him in the air. The skeletal old man bounced like a rubber ball on the grass bank.

Just as Chughtai was also getting ready to pounce on the old man, a crowd suddenly materialized from God knows where and began to hem us in from all sides. The speed with which they scrambled to the scene made us believe that they were expecting a showdown—indeed they were spoiling for it. Instead of picking up the haggard old man from the ground, they moved ominously toward us.

"Get out of here. Quick! Or else, brace yourselves for a riot!" Rahman Sahib whispered, pushing us to one side. But there was no getting away. The mob was steadily closing in on us. Rahman Sahib dashed to the side where the crowd looked thicker and began to rattle off in Bengali.

But not one soul was listening to his words which were dissolving into the air like a fine vapor. They were talking all at once and moving closer and closer toward us. "Hitting a poor, old *madman*, huh? Don't you have any shame?"

"What? Madman? he is *not* mad!"

Suddenly the old man reappeared and installed himself right in front of us again. "Don't you know I am Lincoln?" he screamed, "Abraham Lincoln?"

"What did he say—Lincoln? . . . Of course!" In spite of the situation, we broke into ringing laughter.

Yusuf Zai quickly moved up close to the old man, patted his hand and said in a perfectly serious voice, "I am awfully sorry, Mr. President, I am truly sorry."

Chughtai, too, had forgotten all about his aching neck and was laughing hilariously with us. But the old man didn't find it funny. He looked grave, and so did Rahman Sahib and the mob. The old man contemptuously pushed Yusuf Zai's hand away, waved his fist in their air and clamored in English, "*No Slavery!*"

We spotted an opening in the mob and began to slip away. "What a weird fellow!" we exclaimed.

"What madman isn't weird?"

"But what the hell's he raving about? Slavery—what slavery?"

"He's mad, after all. What are you getting so irritated about . . ."

Rahman Sahib didn't say a word. He just kept walking along. This was his own city. He had lived here for the past twenty-three years. And he had come to receive us at the railway terminal.

Rahman Sahib's little Fiat turned the corner and we saw that the whole mob was now waving its fists ominously in the air along with the old man.

They called the joker the "turtle." And that woman with full, fleshy lips got at least two jokers every deal. She would lick her lips with her blood-red tongue and coat them a deep red as well, as I brooded over the advantages of chewing betel leaf, so common in Bengal: it certainly made your lips look voluptuously red. Dangerous, too. And this "turtle" was strange creature: sensing the slightest danger, how it pulled its head back into the shell and froze on the spot. But why do these people call a joker a turtle?

Those full, fleshy red lips had managed to clean everyone's pockets, even Yusuf Zai's who was otherwise known to be an accomplished card player. He just kept looking dumbly at us with his big, innocent eyes, as aghast as a sacrificial lamb. The Divisional Forest Officer was bursting with pride at his wife's smashing performance, breaking every now and then into loud applause: "She's marvelous! Husna is simply terrific!"

"Endless rhapsodies about her delightfully tawny complexion, her incredibly melodious body. Bah! Propaganda, just plain propaganda and lies. You get so psyched up hearing those litanies you begin to see the lousiest wench warbling a bhatyali." Yusuf Zai, who had for a whole fortnight not once seen the slightest ray of hope, finally vented his frustration on the much touted charms of Bengali women.

"Abject poverty and hunger—what else do you expect? Give them enough to eat and then see how they blossom, how the deathly dark color leaps into a vibrant complexion." Rahman Sahib had an answer for everything.

"Nonsense. Well, all right. So you can improve the complexion, but what about her features? How are you going to knock them into shape? Haven't you noticed: if the lips are beautiful, the nose is hidious—plain ugly; and if the eyes are lovely, the lips are weird-looking? Even her celebrated eyes aren't all that beautiful, either. That is, if you cared to look closely."

"You've got to jump into the river to see how deep it is."

"Don't give me that. I've had quite few jumps already."

"Cross-breeding—that's the answer. That's it."

"So you want us to marry them—is that it? Those shriveled mummies? Just for a pair of beautiful eyes. Forget it! Who wants to sire a whole generation of freaks?"

"Who said anything about marrying them? But, I'd . . ."

"So what else is new?"

Rahman Sahib was very perturbed. Rahman Sahib who was a Bengali, and then again not; one who backed us up, but who also backed up Jalil Bhai; who wished to offend neither us nor Jalil Bhai; who quarreled with us, just as he quarreled with Jalil Bhai; who looked to us for help, just as he looked to Jalil Bhai; and who, finally, understood neither our point of view nor Jalil Bhai's. Whenever a surge of love for Rahman Bhai swept across Yusuf Zai, he would pick up his diminutive, slight body, and waltz him all over the deck.

"When I set up a grand hosiery factory here, you know what? I'll make Rahman Sahib the General Manager."

"Hosiery? But only yesterday you were talking about setting up a jute mill."

"Well, you see, it's like this: none of the locals seem to wear shirts; all they ever wear are undershirts. A hosiery business will do well. Don't you think? They'll profit from it, and so will *we*."

"What about your plans for the bicycle factory?"

'That's good business, too. But where will I get the raw material for bicycles? Let bicycles come from West Pakistan. What do you think, Rahman Sahib?"

But Rahman Sahib didn't care to reply; he always preferred silence whenever discussion veered to controversial matters. Only Yusuf Zai and Chughtai evinced a strong interest in them.

"Our people are very poor," said Atiquzzaman Khan, pushing a mug of chilled beer toward his brother Amiruzzaman Khan in "Saqi"—the bar in Hotel Intercontinental.

"His pronunciation," Chughtai whispered into my ears, "it seems all right—doesn't it?"

It was afternoon. A young Bengali couple, beer mugs in hand, was talking in undertones at the table directly across from us.

"What I can't understand is . . ." Chughtai took a big gulp of beer and shut up.

"What don't you understand?"

"Nothing. Nothing at all."

"You know why? Because you are perched up too high on your loft. How can you!"

"Or perhaps you don't try to understand it at all," Amiruzzaman Khan was quick to remark in English.

Chughtai observed that the two brothers' pronunciation was atrocious after all.

"How can I? Yes, how can I?"

Amiruzzaman Khan had kept asking me a great deal about the folksongs of Multan and Bahawalpur regions; he had even promised to come to Multan to tape them. I just gazed quietly at the low ceiling of the "Saqi" and the smart-looking bartender behind the counter.

"Yes, our people are very poor," said the Divisional Forest Officer of Khulna, who had, since Atiquzzaman was paying, already guzzled down two mugs of beer.

"And so are our people," Chughtai shot back as he jumped a little from his chair and stared the Forest Officer full in the face. "They are very poor, too."

"*No!* We are poorer still. Really poor. No comparison."

"In poverty," Yusuf Zai tried to reconcile the two, "we are all equals. We are one."

"No! We are not *equals*. Nor are we *one.*"

"Dera Ghazi Khan, Mianwali, Sirhad, Baluchistan, Thar . . ."

But what were we fighting about? And why? The Forest Officer had invited to show us around Sundarbans. We must try to make him feel comfortable and happy. So I glared at Yusuf Zai, he at Chughtai, and the three of us shut up. But now the three of them had started to talk. And in Bengali at that. We felt isolated. We sat in their midst, but obviously we were not one of them. Suddenly a deluge of voices filled the entire hotel and the bar. The mouths of Atiquzzaman Khan, Amiruzzaman Khan, and the Forest Officer began to open and shut with such frightening speed that I felt giddy and emptied the whole mug in one giant, nervous gulp.

Then, at last, we were on the river. We disturbed the waters hurling coconut husks at assorted targets, then aimed the husks at the butterflies and, somewhere along the line, got thirsty. Jalil Bhai picked out five coconuts from the bucket, took out a long, thin knife, and hacked one.

"Agh! Stop it, Jalil Bhai! It's sheer murder. Why are you killing them off so coldbloodedly?"

Jalil Bhai's hand froze. He looked at Chughtai with malicious eyes, but Chughtai gave an undaunted laugh and picked up a bottle of beer from the pail. Then he said, "Khan-ji, go get a glass. Let's give Jalil Bhai something different for a change."

But Jalil Bhai quickly sucked at the split coconut and downed all the milk in one hasty gulp. Rahman Sahib, to keep Jalil Bhai's morale high, picked a coconut himself. Just as he was getting ready to slash it open, Yusuf Zai snatched the fruit from his hand and tossed it outside toward the Forest Guard, "Here, catch!"

We had been cruising around in the boat from one river port to the next for two whole days and still we had hardly put a dent in the supply of beer and coconuts. The heap had hardly diminished; on the contrary, it seemed to be growing bigger and bigger.

"Why on earth did we have to haul these coconuts along?"

"To make you happy and to win over the hearts of Jalil Bhai and the Forest Guard—I suppose."

"So?"

"So, nothing."

"Well, then drink them!"

"We will, we will. After we've run out of the beer."

But it seemed the beer would outlast us. Jalil Bhai's mood was getting worse. Was he upset because he couldn't get us to drink coconut milk or because he couldn't put up with Yusuf Zai puttering around in the engine compartment—we couldn't tell. Every time Yusuf Zai tinkered with the engine and sped up the boat, Jalil Bhai got jittery all over and shouted, "Mr. Yusuf Jai, let my men take care of the boat. Don't monkey around."

"But Jalil Bhai I can pilot a boat too. No big deal. In fact, I can pilot it even better . . ."

"No, mister, I won't let you mess around with it. No! Only my man will pilot it."

"Huh? The hell he will!" Yusuf Zai would come over and sit beside us, still fuming, "The sonofabitch hardly has an ounce of flesh left on his body—the hell he will. The bastard keeps dozing off the whole day long."

When petty quarrels broke out over coconuts and beer, Jalil Bhai quietly withdrew to his cabin and immersed himself in his books. He had brought along quite a few and stuffed them in the small cabinet above his berth. In vain would I try to tell them that beside beer and coconut milk there was also such a thing as water; but they wouldn't listen. Jalil Bhai would quickly disappear behind his book and Chughtai would begin to warble a Nazrul song: "*Chol, chol, chal . . .*"

I believe it was Friday. The front of Bait al-Mukarram was filled with people who stood in sundry, large groups. The man who drew the biggest crowd was hawking amulets. He couldn't have been a smarter salesman. From one for ten paisas to one for fifty paisas—you name it, there was an amulet for everybody. And people were buying them with perfect humility and unswerving faith.

"What a paradox!"

"Paradox! What paradox?" Rahman Sahib couldn't understand any of it. For him this was nothing strange, nothing paradoxical at all. Everything was proceeding with perfect smoothness. Normal—period.

"All the same, it is a profitable business," Yusuf Zai said. Moments later he plunged into the crowd, elbowing his way to the hawking peddler.

"Well, I'll tell you: on one hand you have a hoary old man shouting slogans to end slavery, and on the other slavery is being given a shot in the arm—that's the paradox."

"You'll never understand *that*, you just can't."

"Why can't I?"

"But Rahman Sahib, we thought every Bengali was a potential revolutionary?"

"Miyan-ji, do you sell an amulet for *inqilab*, too?" Yusuf Zai, who had probably caught Chughtai's remark, moved forward and asked the old vendor with studied seriousness.

By now Chughtai, Rahman Sahib and I had inched our way to the very first row and were directly facing the Pir Sahib. The Pir Sahib ignored Yusuf Zai's question and, his head bent low, went on selling amulets to people who sat squatting on the ground. Yusuf Zai repeated the question, only this time he didn't use the word "inqilab" but the English word "revolution." Still Pir Sahib didn't care to look up and continued to be busy in his work.

Rahman Sahib tried to nudge Yusuf Zai away from the scene, but the latter had dug in, and wasn't about to be budged. A playful Chughtai was constantly egging him on, "Come on, buddy, ask him again."

"For God's sake, Chughtai Sahib, why must . . ."

"Oh, no, Rahman Sahib, I'm just joking. Can't the Pir Sahib see that? Surely, he can take a bit of sport."

Frustrated in his third attempt also, Yusuf Zai tried to solicit Rahman Sahib's help. "What is the word for inqilab in Bengali?" he asked.

But Rahman Sahib—whether because Yusuf Zai had angered him with his antics or because he had become really scared of what might follow, we couldn't tell—quickly withdrew from the scene. Only I remained standing behind Yusuf Zai and volunteered, *"Kranti."*

"What?" Yusuf Zai couldn't figure out the word.

"Kranti! Kranti!" I shouted, loud and clear, and before I knew it, the entire crowd had suddenly dropped their business with the Pir Sahib and was beginning to surround us. They were staring at us so hard it looked as though they would eat us alive. I turned around to locate Rahman Sahib. He had vanished without a trace.

And then it seemed as though suddenly all the bands of people from Jinnah Avenue to Bait al-Mukarram had started to press in on us, trying to crush us with the weight of their collected bodies. I looked at the flight of stairs leading up the Bait al-Mukarram; maybe—just maybe—a single hand might rise in our defense. Bu the stairs only offered an unbroken view of a ferocious tidal wave of heads from which all hands had ominously disappeared.

A confused Yusuf Zai was looking sheepishly at the crowd and snickering to lessen his embarrassment, while Chughtai comically jabbered on in his pidgin Bengali, proffering a hand of friendship which nobody in the crowd seemed prepared or willing to accept. The mob's eyes were glued, instead, on his big, jutting, Pathan nose and a broad forehead.

Suddenly my eyes fell upon the face of the Pir Sahib who had, God knows when, come and planted himself right in front of me. "Chughtai." I screamed, "it's the same mad man we saw in Chittagong!"

Chughtai and Yusuf Zai, too, turned around to look at the man and let out a wild scream, "Run!"

And we ran, tearing our way through the surging crowd. Chughtai had scrambled off towards Bait al-Mukarram. Yusuf Zai and I followed suit. But the stairs of Bait al-Mukarram seemed endless. Soon our legs buckled from fatigue and we crumbled on the steps.

I wanted to talk. I wanted to talk about many things, so many things that I wished everyone in the cabin cruiser would just stop their work and come over and listen to me, listen to what I had to say, to things whose oppressive weight was crushing my chest. I wanted to lighten this weight . . . and the weight of all the things that were weighing heavily upon them as well. But they were preoccupied with their own work. They had no time for me. Rahman Sahib was getting the "dispatch" ready for his newspaper, Chughtai was quarrelling with the Forest Guard over a suitable, cool spot to store the pail of chilled beer, Yusuf Zai, having failed to interest anyone in playing rummy, had withdrawn to a quiet corner and occupied himself with solitaire, and Jalil Bhai was doing God knows what shut up inside the engine compartment.

Why don't these people ever sit together? Why are they so keen on keeping away from each other? Oh how I wish this boat stopped for a while—even in the middle of the river! Perhaps then things might change, or they might not . . . who knows? The waters of the river are muddy, the surface is riddled with *jal-kumri* plants. And the area is infested with crocodiles—they say. What if the jal-kumri were to spread over the entire river? How would the boats move, then? One could have asked all these questions of Jalil Bhai, if only he had been around on the deck, but he couldn't have picked a worse time to worry about the engine.

Husna Begum won the hand again and the Forest Officer's un-bounded adulation burst forth in cries of "Marvelous! Terrific!" And then, all of a sudden, a naked, starving Bengali cropped up from God knows where. They began to compare him to the starving and naked of Dera Ghazi Khan in West Pakistan. I just kept my eyes fixed on those juicy red lips which appeared totally motionless, while the rest of them kept hurling question after blind question at one another. Whenever I took my eyes off those lips, it was only to look for a joker in the cards I held. But I didn't get a joker in a single hand. By now my tongue had become so dry and thick I could scarcely move it over my parched lips.

"Our man works for four annas. Imagine, just four annas. And yours for a whole *taka*—I mean a whole rupee."

"A rupee? No. More like four." Rahman Sahib quickly corrected the Forest Officer. "Yes, yes, four rupees, yes," the Forest Officer, who had traveled through West Pakistan, said. His wife, however, had only dreamed of Karachi and Lahore; so the very mention of those cities and a bare glance at our colorful, expensive clothes was enough to set her eyes agleam.

"Husna Begum's eyes are truly lovely."

"That they are. But in a different face they'd look even lovelier."

After breakfast it was Chughtai who became impatient about the boat trip and asked, "When will the darn thing get moving?"

"Mr. Zalil will be along soon. We'll leave as soon as he comes. Meantime, you get ready."

This was the first time when this pronunciation of "Jalil Bhai" had brought us to the verge of laughter; Chughtai had quickly pinched his nose to keep from laughing—the sudden onrush of blood dyeing his eyes a deep red—and Rahman Bhai had whirled around and glowered at us in irritation.

Finally, Jalil Bhai arrived. Introductions followed. The stuff we were bringing along began to be packed: three suitcases, a huge burlap sack stuffed with coconuts, and a wooden case of bottled beer. The coconuts were a gift from the Forest Officer and his wife. ("You won't get drinking water on the river; so use them when you get thirsty," the couple had said.) The beer was the common property of Yusuf Zai, Chughtai, and myself.

"Look fellows, this isn't proper," said Rahman Bhai, who was lounging in a cane chair inside the room watching us pack for the trip ahead.

"What isn't proper?" Chughtai asked, flabbergasted, as he threaded a pair of expensive cufflinks in his silk shirt.

"That you keep mocking these people all the time."

"For God's sake Rahman Bhai, just tell us who we've mocked?"

"Then there is such a thing as a sense of humor, too."

"Khan Sahib," Rahman Sahib began with some irritation, "you are now in Bengal. You must really try to accept its ways."

"Are you going to tell me that you have?" Chughtai shot back, emerging from the bathroom.

"Yes, *I have.*"

"You mean there is no difference between how you live and how the average Bengali lives?"

Rahman Sahib became speechless. He looked out of the window for a while, picked his way to the door, but then stopped short. "When we were new here," he began, lighting the cigarette pressed between

Chughtai's lips, "an amusing thing happened to us. We employed a young Bengali girl to help us out with house work . . ."

"A young girl—wow!"

"Yes, about seventeen or eighteen years old." Rahman Sahib sank back into the cane chair. "She never wore a blouse, though . . ."

"No blouse?" Yusuf Zai cut in, jumping up. "You mean altogether nude? God be praised!"

"Well, she'd just wrap herself in a gauze-like muslin sari . . ."

"How much of her could she possibly have wrapped in a sari . . ."

"That's just it. It bothered us a lot, especially my wife . . ."

"I bet it did, you being a strapping youth and all that. Your wife had to . . ."

"Anyway, my wife got her a few blouses and ordered her to put one on."

"What a pity. She should've left her alone."

"Yes, what a pity. She somehow endured the blouse for a day, but the very next day she ran away."

"Ran away? You mean she quit?"

"Yes, she quit. Nobody in her entire family had so much as ever dreamed of wearing a blouse."

"Makes sense. She didn't want to be cooped up inside a blouse."

"Oh, there was more. Her family thought it plain indecent to wear a blouse. It meant that the girl was whoring around."

"My goodness!"

"You didn't look for another servant girl?"

"Oh yes, we did."

"One without a blouse?"

"Wow, Rahman Sahib, you must have had lots of fun."

Suddenly there was a loud crash outside, followed by the screams of the Forest Officer. We were so shocked we just stood staring dumbly at one another for some time. All at once, Rahman Sahib shot out of the room. We followed. In the veranda we all came to a sudden halt.

A beer bottle lay shattered on the floor, and in the middle of a pool of spilled beer stood a hoary old man with nothing on except a rag of checked cloth wrapped around his waist. He stood with his back to us, supporting the wooden case of beer on his left shoulder, as rivers of sweat gushed down from the upper half of his naked body. His head was hung very low, and with his right hand he was rubbing his cheeks embarrassedly. Nearby the Forest Officer was wringing his hand and shouting at the old man in Bengali.

"Never mind," Yusuf Zai said, moving a bit forward. "He just broke *one* bottle."

"No, sir. These lazy bums never do anything well. They'd rather die of starvation than work. And when, for a change, they do work, they always botch it."

The Forest Officer screamed again at the old man. Rahman Sahib and even Husna Begum, who had meanwhile walked in, started saying something to the old man in Bengali.

The scrawny old man shifted the case from his left to his right shoulder, turned around and looked at us. Suddenly we, who weren't Bengalis, cringed from a stab of shame.

"Oh, no! He's here, too!"

"Be quiet!"

We became quiet and remained so until we had boarded the boat and Yusuf Zai had dealt out the cards for a game of rummy.

"Bengal is truly a land of magicians!"

"Huh! We shall never accept the slavery you force upon us, though we wouldn't mind being mistreated by one of our own . . ."

"We want the right to slap *our* people with *our* hands."

"Bravo!"

We sailed past one quay, then another; downed three beers, then six; split coconuts and fed their milk to the Forest Officer, Jalil Bhai, Rahman Sahib, and the Forest Guard; and tossed some coconuts into the river.

Suddenly it hit me with brutal clarity that all these people were somehow drifting farther and farther away from me; as if there were two separate boats, not one; that they were aboard one and we aboard the other; and the two boats were headed in opposite directions.

I was afraid. I was afraid of being left alone. I did not want to be left alone. I looked at all those very busy people once again and picked my way to the small cabinet above Jalil Bhai's berth in search of an understanding companion. Why not talk to books? Yes . . .

But those books, too, did not know my language. Tagore, Madhusudan Das, Nazrul Islam, Munir Chaudhury, Shahidullah Qaisar—all neatly lined up before me but unable to understand me. Of course I recognized these authors from their pictures on the dust covers; they, too, perhaps, recognized me by me face. I couldn't understand what they were saying; I was just looking over the titles, leafing through the pages—dumbly. It was all useless; no one knew my language, not one could talk with me. Then, my eyes fell upon a book that knew me, that also knew Jalil Bhai—indeed it knew us both at the same time. It was *The Spy Who Came in from the Cold.*

I left the cabin.

Evening mist blurred the edges of the river, as a weary sun slipped into its waters. Or, was it perhaps rising from the river? Was it evening? Morning? Sunrise? Sunset? I couldn't tell.

Husna Begum's voice was assaulting my ears. Was she also on the boat, then? I heard the voices of Atiquzzaman Khan and Amiruzzaman Khan as well. And the Forest Officer, too. It seemed they were all aboard the boat—indeed it seemed all of Bengal had scrambled aboard the boat, which was rocking perilously.

"Rahman Sahib . . . Rahman Bhai . . . Where have you run off to? And you, too, Jalil Bhai? How on earth have these people managed to jump aboard right in the middle of the river? Didn't the jal-kumri block their way? And the crocodiles—millions of crocodiles, who rule the river waters—didn't they scare them off . . . Rahman Sahib . . . Rahman Dada . . ."

Rahman Sahib was nowhere to be found. Somehow I knew—as certainly as I knew that I existed—that Jalil Bhai was lurking somewhere nearby. Had Rahman Sahib been around, he surely would have responded to our urgent pleas and rushed to help us.

The entire boat was filled with people: swarthy, cadaverous Bengalis crowding in the engine compartment, cabins, the small deck—everywhere. It was impossible to tell them apart. I quickly hid Chughtai and Yusuf Zai behind me and desperately looked around in the crowd for the benign faces of Husna Begum and Atiquzzaman Khan, but couldn't find them. They, too, had become lost in the crowd—or, perhaps, become part of it. I could only hear their voices, which were so distant I couldn't make out what they were saying.

"Where in the hell has Rahman Sahib run off to?" And then I screamed, pulling all the strength out of my lungs: "Rahman Sa-a-a-hib!"

"The boat had become too damn heavy . . ." came the answer from someone standing close by, who spoke ominously and with slow deliberation.

I turned around to see who it was. "My god!" I shrieked, "You again?"

" . . . and still *is*."

Translated by Muhammad Umar Memon

Saleem Asmi

Fire, Ashes and Water

SALEEM ASMI

Annima, our *ayah*, opened the door, and we all walked in. She said, "You're all going to catch pneumonia. Go dry your hair and change clothes. The fire is lit in the sitting room. Go." And she added, "Grown up girls and look . . ." Bajiya looked at me. Her long hair was dripping water. Her shirt had clung to her body and she stood almost naked. Her moccasins were full of water; and Sophia, too, was naked. My mind is sick, I confess. My older sister always seems naked to me. Bajiya looked at me, and (*Annima said, "Come out of the trunk right now; come, you are no longer a little girl." And she said, "Saffo, you too, or I'll go tell your mother. Such grown up girls and look at them," and she said, "No sense of shame at all." Bajiya looked at me. Saffo did too, and Bajiya said, "Annima, you are a bastard and a pig's offspring," and Saffo said, "Annima, you have gone mad." Her naked body was dripping water. There was a pool of water around her feet and her long hair was soaked in water. Bajiya said, "Come out Saffo. We'll go lie down in bed," and Saffo too came out of the trunk. Golden fish appeared from behind the rocks, out of the trunk, and they were all naked*) Bajiya said to me, "Why don't you ever take off this moldy sweater? You look like a mouse. You have just gotten over typhoid. Who asked you to come with us to get yourself killed?" And Annima said, "Don't tease him too much."

Annima opened the door and we all walked inside. Annima said, "You are all sucking my blood. Mother started crying. She pushed the wheelchair near the fireplace and began weeping, and she said, "You two are sucking my blood." Annima shoved a few more pieces of kindling into the fire. The screen lying beside the fireplace became red, and the flames began to dance on the four pictures hanging on the wall. Father's lips began to move, so did Sibbi's. Mother's face grew red: her white shawl also grew red, and so did Bajiya's body—My mind is sick, and my body is sick too. Then Saffo lifted the bottoms of her *shalvar* up to her knees, and mother began crying.

"Begum, why do you cry so? Already you are not well." But mother kept on crying, and said, "This witch is devouring me. O God, take me away from this place, this blasted house."

Annima said, "Begum you shouldn't be crying so. You are not well." Mother wiped her nose with the end of her shawl, and Saffo said, "Now I am going home."

Mother said, "Tell this bitch to get out of my sight. Why does she not die and end my troubles? Tell her I'll skin her alive if she goes in the water again." Bajiya looked at me and Saffo did too. Her white calves were naked. Her shirt clung to her body, and her hair dripped water, and her body was red, and Bajiya's eyes were red. Bajiya said, "I will go in the water, I will, I will, I will."

And mother started crying again. "Tell this bitch to get away from here," she said, and Bajiya said, "I will not, I will not, I will not go," and she sat down on the carpet stretching her feet. Her shalvar was sticking to her legs and her shirt to her torso and she was completely naked. Then she took off her (*Bajiya said "Get down; now it is my turn to get on the swings." Annima said, "Why are you bothering him?" but Bajiya insisted, "It is my turn." So Annima took me off the swing and Bajiya stood on the plank. The wind got into her frock which turned over, and Bajiya was naked. Annima said, "Swing slowly," but Bajiya's frock went further up; my mind is sick*) shirt, and mother started crying. (*Behind the hedge the two of them were playing badminton. Annima said, "Yes, you may go to the hedge. I'll wait for you on the steps. Don't go far; you are still weak." Behind the hedge they played badminton. Bajiya said, "Saffo, you also take it off; it is so hot," and Saffo took off her blouse. Her white body flashed out of her black bodice. Then Bajiya took off her bodice as well, behind the hedge. "Come back, Salloo," Annima called me, and Bajiya took off her bodice as well. Her bare body was perspiring and glistening in the sun. So was Saffo's. Then they lay down on the cool green grass, behind the hedge. Bajiya's white shorts stuck tightly to her hips, and Saffo's white legs were naked, and the two lay on the grass. Behind the hedge. "Salloo, son, come on. It is getting late," Annima held me by the arm. Then she said to Bajiya, "What is going on? Have you lost all shame? In front of your own younger brother . . ." and Bajiya said, "Who the hell do you think you are? Bastard. Bitch," and Annima said, "Salloo, go in." Then we came inside. Bajiya and Saffo remained behind the hedge, but we came inside*) Mother started crying.

Then mother beckoned me to her and put my head on her lap. The rings on her fingers glittered, and her paralyzed leg quivered continually, and her whole body was shaking. Then Annima said, "Begum, why are you crying?"

Then Annima put a blanket around me, and I was in darkness, a warm darkness. Mother's lap was hot like a furnace. Between her paralyzed leg and her healthy leg, my nose began to grow big. It became as large as Bajiya's middle finger. Then, in that darkness, it seemed as if someone had put a warm, wet and sticky glove on it, between mother's healthy and paralyzed legs, and I began to suffocate. Mother said "Lord, take me back. What sins of mine am I paying for? You are my only hope. When will this witch get off my chest? She doesn't even die."

"Begum why do you go on crying?" And mother said, "Your father has left me all alone to bear all these troubles. God is my only hope now. Oh, I wish Sibbi were alive, but this witch devoured him." (*Annima said, "I am tired of giving you baths. As soon as it rains, you jump in the mud. This damned house is a forest." And my older brother said to Bajiya, "Come out of the pit or I am going to spank you hard," and Annima said, "Tch, tch, how shameful; step out of it," and my brother said, "Come out or else," but Bajiya said, "I will not, I will not." Then my brother pulled her out by her hair. Bajiya started crying, and I cried, and my brother said, "Shut up, or I am really going to hit you." and Bajiya said, "Pig! Bastard!" then my brother picked Bajiya's frock up from the ground and threw it towards her. "Put it on," he said, "Put it on," but Bajiya threw the frock in the mud. My brother threw her on the ground and sat on her, and the mud clothes she was wearing became tattered and began peeling off and flying in all directions, and she became naked, and her legs began kicking in the air. Annima pulled him off her. Then she ran towards the rocks.*) "Yes, this witch has killed him. Why doesn't someone abduct her?" The grip of the hot, wet and sticky glove on my nose started becoming tighter and I couldn't breathe. Then the blanket slipped off my head, and mother's lap became cold, and there was light in the room once again. Bajiya was lying on the carpet, and Saffo's shalvar had been drawn back a little further on her legs, and Bajiya was on the carpet. Saffo said, "It is getting late. I must go home now." (*Then the two of them lay down on the grass, behind the hedge.*) And mother began crying.

"Begum, why do you go on crying?" And mother said, "The evil witch," and Bajiya said, "Mother, you are crazy," and mother started crying, and Saffo said, "Now I am leaving," and Bajiya said (*Then Bajiya ran towards the rocks, and my brother bit Annima on her arm, and then he too ran towards the rocks, and Annima said, "Come back right now, both of you, or*

*I'm going to call your father," and my brother ran to the rocks . . . Then Annima,
too, ran to the rocks, and I began crying),* "You have lost your mind, mother.
I am the master of this house. Only what I want will happen here.
Father made me the master. If I do not want to marry, I will not marry.
If I want to go in the mud, I will go in the mud. Whether I go naked or
dressed-up, it is my will. Whoever does not like to watch me can shut his
eyes. I don't care. I am the master here. Father made me so. You are
going crazy. This bastard Annima is addling your brains. One day I am
going to throw her out of the house. I can do that whenever I want to,"
and mother said, "This witch will be the death of me. She'll be the
death of everyone in this house one day." (*Then Annima ran towards the
rocks. Then Bajiya came running back from the rocks and went inside the house.
Then Annima came back from the rocks. She was carrying my brother on her
arms in such a way that half of his body fell back on her shoulders like a towel,
and that towel had blood stains on it. Annima's shoulder too had blood stains on
it. Then Annima went inside the house. I started crying and mother started
crying. Then Bajiya installed herself proudly in father's lap, and father said,
"You are crazy. You are crying as if the whole family has perished. Look these two
are alive, and this one is my own lovely girl," and mother said, "This witch ate
him up," and Bajiya said, "I'm not a girl," and father said, "Of course, you are
my son. I had three sons; two of them are still here. Your mother is crazy to be
crying like that." Then he said, "Soon I'll hang Sibbi's picture on the wall. My
own picture will be there one day, and yours too, but this house will go on. There
is nothing to cry about, is there, son?" and Bajiya said, "I am a boy, isn't that so,
Abbu?" and father said, "When your grandfather built this house and purchased
the mango orchard and the canal-irrigated land, he reserved this wall for pictures. He hung your grandmother's picture there. I hung his and will now hang
Sibbi's, and you'll hang my picture there," and Bajiya said, "But I am not a
girl,"—and she lifted her frock and said, "Look Salloo, I piss like boys," and my
brother pulled her to the ground by her hair and her frock went up a little further,
and she said, "Bhaijan, idiot, son of a pig?—and Bajiya said, "I am not a girl,"
and father said, "That's why your grandfather built this wall. In winter when the
fire is lit, the lips of the people in the pictures begin moving, and these pictures say
to you that life is a lovely thing. One should not spend it crying, but your mother
is crazy. She goes on crying."*) And mother said, "This witch will kill us all,"
and Saffo said, "Now I am going home," and Bajiya said, "I own everything here," and mother began crying. The flames danced in her tear-
filled eyes, and they danced on the pictures on the wall. (*Father said,
"Life is lovely"*) and mother said, "Life is hell," and Annima said, "Begum,

you should not be crying," and Saffo said, "I am going home now." Then she pulled the bottoms of her shalvar down, and it became dark in the room. (*Father put my brother's picture on the wall and said, "Now there are three pictures here," and mother started crying, and mother said, "You have the heart of a stone," and father said, "I love life. Each one of us has to die so there is nothing to cry about. When my father built this house, he thought there would be twenty people in the family. That's why he built twenty bedrooms and this enormous sitting room which can never be filled up. The more furniture you put in here, the barer it looks. But there were only three people in our house. You were the fourth to come, but again we became three. Then Sibbi came, but my father passed away. We were again three. No, actually we were five, three would walk around and two were permanently on this wall. Then we became six. Then Salloo came and we became seven. Then we were reduced to four—four who could walk around, three having been nailed to the cross of this wall. But still seven all the same. So, in this way, some day all these desolate rooms will fill up and so will this wall. So what is there to cry about?*") And the room became dark again, and Saffo said, "Now I am leaving," and the flames began to dance on the four pictures on the wall, and mother began crying. (*Bajiya said, "Come here, Salloo, I'll show you something," and we went into our parents' bedroom. It was dark in there, and it was raining outside, and Bajiya said, "Look, Salloo, look at Abbu's pipe." His pipe had fallen in his lap, and his dressing gown was burning slowly. His head was rolled on one side, and his eyes were closed, and Bajiya said, "Look Abbu's gown is on fire," and she said, "Look, how he is asleep, with his mouth open." Then I started crying. Bajiya began to cry too. Then mother came in and she too began crying. Then Annima came in, and she too began crying . . . And mother said, "Now who is going to care for me?" and she pulled me to her legs and embraced me and said, "Who is mine in the whole world now," and Annima said, "Begum, bear this patiently," and mother said, "This wretched house is so unlucky," and Bajiya said, "Abbu is dead. Now his picture will go on the wall, won't it, Salloo?" and mother said, "You shut up, you evil witch."*) Mother said, "This witch will destroy us all," and Saffo said, "Now I must leave." Then Bajiya got up from the carpet and picking up her shirt went into the dining room, and Salloo followed her, and Annima said, "Begum, you come too. The food is ready," and began pushing mother's wheelchair. Mother's shawl returned to its original white color when they came out of the sitting-room and Saffo said, "I am not going to eat. I must go," and Bajiya said, "My love, it is only nine o'clock." Now Bajiya had put on her shirt. She never felt cold, nor did Saffo. Then Bajiya said, "This house is so wretched. There is nothing but weeping and wailing here. Nobody can even talk properly to anybody for a minute. I am going to turn everyone out of here. Burn the house down and put everyone's picture on the wall. My father made me the master of this house." Annima said, "Please don't talk like that, daughter," and Bajiya said, "You keep your mouth shut. You are nothing but a lowly servant," and Annima said, "I've raised everyone of you," and she began crying; and mother said, "Please stop crying. You know how mean she is," and Bajiya said, "Go, take Saffo home," and Annima said, "I won't. I have raised each one of you," and Bajiya said, "If people in this house can do nothing but cry all the time, then I'll turn everyone out of here. I'll sell the house, land, orchard, everything. I own everything here, and mother said, "Please go with Saffo, or this wretch will go on roaring like that forever." Then Saffo and Annima went out into the moonlight, beyond the hedge where there was green grass and the badminton court. Then mother said, "I'm not hungry. I do not want to eat," and mother's room was warm, her bed was warm, and so was her body.

I'm dying, my love.

Her fingers kept on dancing.

My love, I'm dying. Each of her fingers had a life of its own. My whole body was on fire. The tips of her fingers gave off incredible heat. Oh, my God, Birjees, my love. I'm dying. Then my body started cooling down, and I began to die. Slowly. Life is beautiful, but death is even more so, especially if Birjees' fingers become its cause. And each of Birjees' fingers is a living, feeling sensing thing; each kills separately, individually, slowly; one does not die suddenly but very slowly. My body started cooling down.

(*Then Salloo began to sweat, and his body went limp. He became sullen and unresponsive, but I was still ablaze. Damn the women folk. Even after surrendering themselves, they cannot be sure what will happen. They worry what will happen if their husbands or lovers turn away from them. Then his body went cold like ice, and the sea-waves stood between us like a massive rampart. Salloo, my love, give me a chance, darling, I need a little help, something that will put out the fire kindled by those fingers. Salloo, my darling.*) My body began to cool down, and I began to die, slowly, but her fingers went on dancing relentlessly.

Birjees, my love. I am dying. Have pity on me (*Annima said, "Talk sense, daughter. What kind of match is this between Saffo and Salloo?"*) Have pity on me, love.

The sea-waves kept dying on the shore (*But Salloo's fingers are dead, too. They do not have enough strength in them to strangle me.*) while Birjees' fingers drain life out of every pore of my body. Oh, this life-giving death at each moment. (*"Talk sense, daughter," Annima said. Birgees said, "Saffo, why won't you take it off? See how hot it is getting." I took off my blouse. Then the two of us lay on the cool green grass. On the other side of the hedge were Salloo and Annima, and Birjees and I were on this side. And there were her fingers. Her breathing, feeling fingers . . . Oh, I'm going to die.*) Let me go now, Birjees. I've bared my very soul to you. Your breath blows on my being like the hot wind of summer, and your fingers have conversed with every pore of my body. Let me and Salloo (*"Will you come to bed, my lord?"*) be together a while longer, o heartless one! my life! my death! or the spacious bedrooms of this massive palace will remain forever desolate, and I'll go on dying minute by minute. Let the woman in me wake up for a while. Birjees, my love, you witch . . .

(*Someone like a shadow walked in the room. My lord and master, body and soul, I'm yours. My whole world is for you. You are my being and my end. But your fingers . . . Why don't you strangle me with them? "Who is there? Othello? Ay, Desdemona. Will you come to bed, my lord?" I put my pillow on my face and it became dark. "To bed, my lord." Then Salloo's breath became normal and my breath started coming in fiery gasps. The pillow became heavy, and I began to suffocate and die. Annima said, "Talk sense, daughter," and Salloo's mother said, "She will kill us all, the witch. I wish Sibbi were alive."*) Birjees' breath, hot and moist, was warming my cheeks, and I was dying.

(*Then Salloo's mother said, "I told you so. She wants to kill Salloo as well." How do you feel now, my lord and master? And Salloo's mother said, "I told so. This witch is going to devour him too." Come, let me give your head a massage. And Salloo's mother said "I knew it. She buried him in her favorite's womb." I beg you. Help me escape those fingers. I need help, not a woman's but a man's. Please help me a little. And Birjees said, "You are crazy, mother. He has always been a weakling, eternally sick. What could Saffo have done to him? He is the unlucky one," and Salloo's mother said, "This wretched one has buried him in her favorite's womb."*) My womb is like a vast graveyard where all the pretty little children have been buried. This is why the bedrooms of this palace are still empty. Your fingers, Birjees, are also lodged there, but they escape time and again and crawl and burrow through my body like heavy ploughs, leaving behind an animal warmth in my womb. A hellish warmth that never subsides.

(*Annima said, "Daughter, come out of the trunk," and Birjees said, "Saffo, you too come out. Let's go and lie down in bed." I looked at Salloo, and Birjees looked at him, and I emerged from the trunk. Birjees' naked body was dripping water, and my naked body was dripping water, and red rays of the warming sun were lifeless on the window-panes, and sighing and gasping. I was dying in the moist bed, slowly—Then Birjees said, "Both of us can get in this tub." She said, "How much fun it is to get soaked in the rain."—Then Annima opened the door and we came in. Then Salloo's mother began crying, and the flames began to dance on the four pictures on the wall, and the dance of Birjees' fingers turned into the windstorm of summer in my womb, and Salloo's mother began crying. Annima opened the door and we walked in.—Then Annima said, "Daughter Saffo, do you also think I'm a servant? I've raised everyone of the children here, Sibbi and Birjees and Salloo. I even fed my milk to Salloo. You don't consider me a servant, do you?"—Behind the hedge it was moonlight and cool green grass. Then we lay down on the green grass, and Birjees said, "Saffo, you take it off too,"—and Annima said, "I am not a servant here, am I? Birjees has been spoiled by her father's love," and she said, "She doesn't even care for her mother's health"—cool green grass—"the poor lady is so sick. You don't talk to your mother like that, do you Saffo?" And Annima said—On the other side of the hedge was the man-eating haunted house; on this side was moonlight and cool green grass. Then Birjees said—and Annima said, "Grown up girls should not stay home unmarried."*) But Salloo's fingers do not have enough strength to strangle me. Someone is walking in the room like a shadow. Who is it? No one. "Will you come to bed? Alas, why gnaw you so your nether lip? Some bloody passion shakes your very frame. Will you, my lord?" Shadow-like, someone walks in the room. Let me go, Birgees, my love. But Salloo's hands do not even press down the pillow on my face to suffocate me. (*Then I put the pillow down on my face, and it became dark, and I began to suffocate. Then his warm breath became cold and mine began to get warm. Salloo, my love, give me a chance. I need your help. I'm burning up. Take me into the rain, throw me into the sea, I want to die, but save me from this fire. I don't want to burn. I cannot stand the crackling sound of my fat melting and burning on the flames. Come, Salloo, love. Bury me in the depth of the sea— Salloo's mother said, "I told you so. This wretched one has buried him in her womb."—My womb is on fire. Salloo, my love, I need your help.*) My womb is a vast graveyard where scorching winds blow at all time, and my soul burns, and I burn and die, slowly, minute by minute.

Someone is walking in the room like a shadow. Who is it? Who is it? No one at all.

No, there is a shadow there. Let me go, witch.

There is no one there.

Who can it be?

No. It's a shadow. Let me go. I am going towards the sea.

Come on, crazy. There is no one else. I am here.

No, there is someone. I want to die. I am dying. Let me go, witch.

Only I am here.

No, it is a shadow. I am leaving now, going to the sea. I shall wrap your head-scarf around my eyes. Walking in the driving rain, I will move on to the sea—where there is fresh green grass, on the other side of the hedge—Let me go, love. Someone walks in the room like a shadow, and there is sea over there where I go. I shall wrap your head-scarf around my eyes and go far riding the crest of waves. Then my body will get heavy and the scaffolding of the waves will collapse. There at the bottom of the sea is fresh green grass. Someone walks again like a shadow.

It is I. Who else, crazy?

No, there is someone else. He has seen us. That's why I am going towards the sea. I want to drown myself in the sea. There is fresh green grass there. Then Birjees said, and we lay down on the fresh green grass. At the bottom of the sea.

One part of the sitting room. There is a fireplace in the wall in front. Many little articles have been set on the mantelpiece. The fire is burning in the fireplace, and the entire sitting room looks as if it were full of red shimmering light. A divan lies on the left of the fireplace, wrapped in a red silken cover. In the light of the fire the red of the silk has assumed a deeper and darker tone. Besides the divan, the sitting room has many diverse things in it, but seeing them one feels as if these things have no connection whatsoever with the outside world, never had, and never will have. The mysterious stillness of the forest hangs on the sitting room, as if there are many sounds there, and then again none at all.

On the wall, to the right of the fireplace, five pictures hang as if they have been tied together. They are all enlarged portraits and have similar black frames. Salloo's father was right in saying, "In winter, when the fire burns in the fireplace, the red flames dance on the surfaces of the pictures and the lips of the people in the pictures begin to move." That's right. The fire burns now, and the flames dance on the pictures, and the lips move, but who knows what those lips say. Salloo's father had said, "These pictures say life is lovely." Maybe that is what they said then. But who knows what they are saying now? Certainly not what Salloo's father claimed. For if you hear someone say that, whether you believe in it or not, your heart does get trapped in the illusion of life's loveliness, and holding the uncertain string of this illusion, you do reach, if for a while, a well-lit place where there is fresh green grass and where birds sing their songs of cheer. In other words, there are some clouds you can recognize, and you know whether they contain a message of joy or eternal wailing and mourning. But now, there, in this sitting room, where red light flickers every where, where you cannot hear anything, where nothing seems to have had or will ever have any connection with the outside world, it is impossible to know what the pictures say. Sometimes you wonder if they say anything, or if their lips move at all. Perhaps it is just the shimmering, moving light. Nothing else moves.

When your gaze disentangles itself from this jungle of furniture and from the confusion caused by the living images trapped within black frames, and you look leftward, you become aware of what is going on in the world outside. (*The world outside?*) Perhaps a storm is raging outside, or it is raining hard. (*Where are Sophia and Birjees now?*) But no. Perhaps it is just the wind, a strong wind, for the curtains of the door and the two windows are flapping violently. The curtain of the door parts and Annima enters. She looks sad. Very downcast. With her white or red head-scarf (*Mother's shawl became red*) she wipes her eyes, and walks to the center of the sitting room. Birjees, sitting on the divan, left of the fireplace, is startled and sits up. See? We were so occupied with this jungle of furniture that we didn't notice Birjees lying on the divan. But this is the way this room is: in this throng of dead things you hardly ever notice the living. With wrath in her eyes, Birjees confronts Annima who, partly scared by Birjees' looks and partly realizing that she is not alone in this jungle, steps back a little.

Birjees: Can I get some peace in this damned graveyard? How many times have I told you to let me die in this corner but . . .

Annima: Daughter, for three days you have lain in this wasteland of a sitting room. Go in your room and have some sleep there, or you too will fall ill like Salloo. You are upsetting Begum Sahiba. Already she does not feel well, and her crying has made her worse. Daughter, would you like some coffee?

Birjees: Why do you care? I have told you a hundred times if I have told you once that I do what I want to do. I am the master of this house and will do with it what I like. You need not interfere. If mother has pampered you, go stay with her. Don't bother me, or I'll really go away, selling this house or setting fire to it. Get lost, do you hear?

It seems Annima wants to say something but does not because she knows Birjees' temperament. Instead, she slowly exits through the left door. It becomes quiet in the sitting room, and behind this sheet of quietness the sun of Birjees' anger sets. She herself sets. The stormy wind is still blowing outside, and the red summer curtains are fluttering, and the shimmering light in the room is red (*Oh God, these reds!*—) The curtain of the door on the left moves again. Perhaps Annima is back. But no, it is Salloo. Salloo is ill (*"Or you too will fall ill like Salloo." A weakling. Eternally sick.*) He is sad. He is crying. He walks straight past the fireplace to the pictures on the wall (*nailed to the corss of the wall*) and cries bitterly. Passing by the fireplace, he too, fails to notice Birjees. Perhaps because of the tears in his eyes. But Birjees sits up on the divan once again. The quivering flames make Salloo's face seem non-human. That does not mean frightening. No, not scary, but ethereal like the faces of beautiful fairies. In the light of the flames his back seems to be shaking. It may really be shaking, for he is sobbing. Birjees gets up, walks toward Salloo, but then suddenly steps back. She watches him in anger and disgust. Salloo is still not aware of her presence. Perhaps the pictures are telling him the way to live. What he couldn't learn from the breathing, walking, living beings, he is perhaps learning from these pictures. Who knows? Perhaps he can understand their language.

Birjees stares at him in anger and with hatred in her eyes. Then she raises the index finger of her hand (*Oh, God, her fingers, each separately living, sensing, feeling and breathing*) as if accusing him.

Birjees: You are an impotent, cowardly murderer.

In embarrassment and fear, he looks at her. His eyes are blood-shot, and his frail body is shaking.

Salloo: I didn't kill her. You know that well, Bajiya. I didn't kill her. She committed suicide. You know that.

Birjees: Impotent, cowardly murderer.

Translated by Faruq Hassan

Intizar Husain

The Seventh Door

INTIZAR HUSAIN

My mother looked upon the pigeon as a holy spirit and made sure that she was not harassed by anyone. Once, when my older brother aimed a slingshot at her, Mother got very upset, snatched at his hand and began to tremble. Her attitude was the result of something that had actually happened to her. One day after she had said her prayers, her eyes closed briefly and she thought she saw a dignified old man, dressed in white, walking casually about the room. She woke up with a start. There was no one in the room except for a pair of small bright eyes shining like stars above the cornice.

Once, I also had a similar experience. Early one morning, I had a dream. I can't remember now what it was about, but it seemed to me that a kind of brilliance, a white glow was leaving the room. I tried to touch it. . . . Just then, I woke up. Mother had unlatched the door and was just stepping out of the room with a jug of water. And just before she crossed the threshold, a bright shadow floated out above her head. All I saw was a ghostly blur and heard the soft flutter of wings.

Mother used to say that in days gone by, there used to be so many pigeons roosting on this cornice that when they flew out in the morning, they darkened the courtyard as though the sky had clouded over.

Once my uncle fired at them with a gun. He only managed to kill one. The others flew away leaving the cornice bare. Mother told us there was a time when our home was full of guests and the kitchen fires burned constantly. But once the pigeons left, misfortune and anxiety wracked our lives and the family scattered to the winds.

Now, all the pigeons are gone. There was only one left. Just one nest on the cornice. Apparently she had decided to desert the flock. She was the mate, perhaps, of the one who had been killed. Her nest was directly across from my bed. The twigs which made up the nest were still there. The cornice was too high for me to reach. Now the nest was empty. But when the pigeon was there, it had looked warm and cozy. At night, I would often wake up and hear the soft rustle of feathers in the dark. Then a silence would descend on the room, and I would drift back to sleep. In the morning when I woke up, the room echoed with the gentle cooing of the pigeon. On summer afternoons when I lay beside my mother, the cooing would lull me to sleep. My eyelids became heavy with drowsiness. But in the winter, this soft cooing served to wake me up and I would glance up at the skylight and see the paleness of dawn through the dusty panes of glass. Then the walls seemed to melt away before the rising waves of the musical murmur and light flooded into the room. Mother would begin to stir. She'd rise, pick up a jug of water and head for the door. As soon as she opend it, the soft, white brilliance spread everywhere. This had a magical effect on the pigeon. She would stretch out her neck, do a little pirouette and then fly out the door with a loud flap-flapping of wings. For a minute or so, she'd perch on the parapet and then she'd be gone, way past the distant rooftops. At dusk, just before the muezzin gave the call for evening prayers, she would reappear on the same parapet. She looked tired, as though she had traveled hundreds of miles. She would be carrying a twig in her beak. She would fly into the room very carefully, and in the gathering darkness, one could hear the sound of her cooing which was like the sound of a bubbling brook. And when she settled into her nest, one could hear a muffled rustling like the murmur of leaves in a gentle breeze. And then—silence.

During the day, one almost forgot she was there on the cornice. Once in a while, I would see the glimmer of a pair of bright eyes. She sat quietly on her nest of dried twigs as though she were mourning for someone.

I believed what mother had told me. This was certainly no pigeon. Perhaps she was a holy spirit. Mother could not possibly have seen a false dream; in fact, what she had seen was not a dream at all.

So when my cousin, Munni, announced that she didn't think the pigeon was a holy spirit, I was rather shocked.

My aunt had arrived only a few days earlier. I had no difficulty recognizing her. Mother took me to her house, telling me that I had to greet her since she was my aunt. She made no mention of Munni. It was all a little embarrassing because she was decked out in fancy clothes whereas mine were rather shabby. My pant-cuff was torn and my shirt had ink spots. Even my face was smudged whereas Munni's was very fair . . . Anyway, I didn't say a word. I just sat there beside my mother for the longest time. Munni seemed tall to me. But then my Aunt told us that we had been born in the same year.

That may or may not have been true. She looked tall to me. Anyway, I never spoke to her. Next day when she came to our house, it was she who started the conversation. I showed her my red and blue pencil, my paint box and my collection of cowries. I would have showed her the pigeon's nest, but she spotted it herself.

"Look! A nest!" she cried out happily.

I said, "Yes. It's a pigeon's nest."

The pigeon, fully alert by now, turned about and flew out at once with a loud clatter of wings.

"It flew away," said Munni excitedly.

In my simplicity, I said to her, "Let her go. She is bound to come back since her nest is here."

"I think we should catch her." She presented a plan.

Alarmed, I timidly said, "No, no. She is a holy spirit."

"A holy spirit!" Munni burst into laughter.

"Yes, a holy spirit," I repeated, a little embarrassed.

"A holy spirit!" She laughed uncontrollably, and a dark curl fell across a rosy cheek.

"Ha, ha, ha . . . holy spirit!"

I was very quiet. "She is a holy spirit, isn't she?"

She stopped laughing and said, "You silly fool. How can a pigeon be a holy spirit? A pigeon is a fairy."

"A fairy?" I said surprised.

"Yes, a fairy. Haven't you heard the story of King Bahram?"

"What of it?"

"You fool," she said playfully, "there was a prince in the story. And the White Giant gave him the keys to all seven doors of the palace, telling him he could open all of them except the seventh door. Every day, the prince opened six doors, looked in and then closed them. But by and by, he got tired of the six doors. He began to wonder why the White Giant had forbidden him from opening the seventh door. Why, what could be behind it? He had to see . . . Finally, he did open the seventh door. What he saw took his breath away—there was a huge pool of sparkling water. And pigeons were diving into the ripples and coming out again all changed into fairies."

I had heard this story from my mother, but it seemed as thought I was hearing it for the first time.

Munni spoke up again, "And among them, there was the green Fairy. And the prince hid her clothes. The Green Fairy stood in the pool naked with her long hair all streaming wet and pleaded with the prince to give her back her clothes. But the prince wouldn't listen."

I began to believe Munni's theory. This pigeon was also a fairy, without a doubt. We decided to find out more. Munni thought that the pigeon went from the parapet onto the roof and there she bathed in dust until she turned into a fairy. And then it flew away on a magic throne.

Next day, Munni came and we waited in the courtyard for the pigeon to emerge. We were then going to follow her to the roof to see what she did. When she did not come out for the longest time, I went in and threw pebbles at her till she flew up. We raced out after her, but by the time we got to the roof, she had vanished.

We were very disappointed. The next day, we waited for her on the roof to see what she would do. She came eventually, but we had to wait a long time. My knees had begun to hurt and my right foot had fallen asleep. In spite of all this, we were not able to discover anything. The pigeon sat on a second-story ledge for a while and flew over us.

"She must have seen us," Munni said sadly.

Eventually, I gave in to Munni's proposal. We concluded that we would never discover the pigeon's secret until we captured her. One afternoon, we shut the door of the room and I got hold of the long bamboo pole with which I used to catch stray kites. I began to strike the cornice with the pole. This startled the pigeon. She left her nest and ran on her delicate pink feet to the far side of the cornice. When I struck the other side with the pole, she ran back. After a few minutes of this, Munni took the pole in her own hands and began to hit the cornice. To tell you the truth, my heart had begun to beat very fast. I couldn't bring myself to use the pole with such violence. But Munni hit the cornice with utter recklessness. The pigeon was very agitated. It flew from the cornice but then, finding the door shut, circled round the room and returned to its nest. But Munni was not about to let it rest. The pigeon flew to the opposite cornice. Her chest heaved with each breath and she glanced about wildly.

Terrified of the thrashing pole, she flew up again and, circling near the girder, alighted on the fan. But the fan began to move and she couldn't stay there. She rose once again and continued to fly around, eventually landing on the skylight. By now, her little grey-feathered body had begun to tremble. She was panting violently. Munni swung the pole once more and the pigeon, unable to rest, rose again only to sink in utter fatigue. She clung to a wall and hung there with her wings and tail feathers spread out while spasms of terror swept over her. Munni slammed the pole again and the pigeon let go of the wall and began to fall. I was ready and went for her even as she fell. She tried to get away, but then, all of a sudden, she stopped, tucked in her neck and tail and turned herself into a little bundle of feathers. I made a quick grab and held her in both hands. Munni grinned joyfully. She threw the pole away and quickly opened the door, yelling, "Bring her into the light." I went towards the door. Something warm quivered in my hands—bright, terrified eyes, a heaving chest, and soft feathers charged with a current of fear. I don't know why, but my heart was so agitated that I relaxed my hold. The pigeon fluttered its wings and flew away.

Munni glared at me with angry eyes. "You let it go?"

I cringed beneath her scolding. I was at fault and I knew it.

The pigeon flew up and sat on the parapet. Perhaps she was catching her breath. I dashed towards the stairs. Munni was right behind me. On the second-story roof, I crouched low and began to move softly toward the parapet. I inched forward till I was very close. I was just about to reach out and grab her when off the pigeon flew with a sudden clatter of wings. I felt awful. I couldn't bring myself to meet Munni's eyes. She gave me the same angry look and left without a word.

I don't know how long I sat near the parapet. The ragged clouds which had been slowly moving across the sky all afternoon had become a solid grey mass. I began to feel cold and went down the stairs in a melancholy mood. When Mother saw me in the courtyard, she called out, "Come in, child. Don't wander about in the cold." When I joined my mother near a glowing charcoal fire, I realized how cold I had been. My teeth were chattering. In a little while, the wind picked up and it began to rain. Mother, my elder brother and my uncle all gathered in the room. My brother closed the door and threw more coals on the fire. A layer of black covered the glowing embers. But pretty soon, they too caught fire and tiny greenish-red flames flared up.

I must have fallen asleep as I sat next to my mother's knee. Late at night when I woke up, I found myself in bed. At some point, mother must have put me to bed. When I woke up the next morning, I sensed that the nest was empty and forlorn. Even the room seemed quiet without the soft musical cooing of the pigeon. Mother rose for dawn prayers, opened the door and stepped out with a jug of water. No grey shadow fluttered past her head. Even then, Mother never suspected that anything was amiss. I lay quietly in bed for the longest time, pondering whether some kid had brought her down with a sling-shot. Then I thought that she may have come back but had then gone away fearful of being harassed.

I could have asked my mother, but I was afraid she should find out what we had done. Until noon, I didn't say a word, acting as if I didn't know anything about the incident. But eventually, I couldn't bear it any longer and questioned my mother. She recalled that the cornice had indeed been quiet that morning and when she had opened the door to go out, no fluttering shadow had gone past her head. And then she remembered that the night before, the door of the room had been closed. For a while, she was lost in deep thought. She was probably wondering if we had shown disrespect to the holy spirit and it had gone away in anger.

In the afternoon, Munni came back. The anger she had felt the day before had more or less subsided. When she heard that the pigeon had not returned, this changed the whole picture. Immediately, we went up to the parapet to look for her. We searched every ledge and cornice. We even climbed up the second set of stairs to the topmost roof. We peered hither and yon, searching the distant roofs, the electricity poles, the nearby *imli* and *neem* trees, but the pigeon was nowhere to be seen.

From where we stood, we could see the temple clearly. It was covered with alcoves and each alcove contained a figurine. As usual, pairs of wild pigeons were sitting in these alcoves. A few were sunning themselves and dozing on the dome. It seemed as though some of them had no necks or heads. Then, all of a sudden, one would poke out its head and do a little dance. In one alcove, a pair was busy kissing. Then the two were locked together and their eyes closed. I was afraid they would fall. But then they separated. Amongst all these pigeons, we couldn't locate ours.

We wearied of looking. Munni sought my eyes, but I did not have the courage to meet her gaze. I stared at the dense imli tree where the pigeons never rested anymore. You could only see an occasional crow or dove. At times, flocks of long-tailed parrots came down in an explosion of screams and then flew away again. Once in a while, a brown-feathered myna bird landed quietly on a branch and then took off. Suddenly, we'd see a bluebird on the highest branch, looking as though he had been there for ages. When we looked again, the branch would be bare and we'd wonder when the bird had flown away. I stared at the tree for the longest time. Munni sat quietly. At length, she said, "You chased her away."

"Why would I do that?" I said, feeling somewhat ashamed as though I really had chased her off.

"Then, do you think I did it?" she snapped angrily.

I did not respond. Neither did she say anything else.

Presently, she spoke up again, "If you think you didn't, then let me hear you swear."

"I won't," I answered irritably.

Munni thought for a second and then said, "He who chased the pigeon is going to burn in Hell."

Hell! This scared me to death. After all, hadn't Munni committed a great sin? I responded quickly, "The person who brought her down with the pole is the one who'll go to Hell!"

My answer angered her so much that she hit me with her elbow. "Get away from me," she said.

This made me mad and I grabbed her hair. She tried to pull away but I wasn't about to let her go. After all, she had been the first to strike. We began to wrestle. All of a sudden, my heart began to pound and a tremor ran through my body. . . . Once again, it seemed as though I had something warm and quivering in my hands, a heaving chest, feathers charged with current . . . I relaxed my hold. She shook me off and went and stood a few feet away. Stray locks clung to her cheeks. She was all disheveled.

She smoothed her hair and glared at me. Then she said, "You don't have any manners," and slowly walked down the stairs. She stopped there briefly. I thought she would look back. She did seem to stop and turn, but then she went down without a backwards glance.

I sat on the roof for the longest time, dazed. The pigeons sat as usual in the alcoves of the temple, cooing and kissing. A male with a black ring around his neck circled round a female, cooing loudly. Then when they heard the sudden noise of a bucket dropping into the temple well, off they flew, up and around swinging in a wide curve, and then settled back in the alcoves.

A crow sat all by itself in the imli tree. Opening his beak, he cawed and cawed. Then growing weary of that, he fell silent. Eventually tiring of just sitting there, he flew away without a sound.

The imli tree stood desolate, its dry seed-pods hanging still.

I sat there for ages. I don't know what I was thinking about. Perhaps nothing. There wasn't anything to think about. My mind was blank. At last, I got tired of sitting on the roof, just got bored by it. I stood up, yawned and headed down the stairs sleepily.

In the evening, Mother made a special point of leaving the door open. I watched the ledge for the longest time, thinking that the pigeon would land there any minute. But she never came. Darkness settled everywhere, and I fell asleep. I woke up many times through the night. And every time I saw that the door was open and the cornice bare. Then I had a dream of sorts in which I caught the pigeon and she turned into a Green Fairy. . . . And Munni walked quietly to the stairs, stopped and then went down without looking back. I woke up with a start. It was early in the morning and the room was filled with light. But the cornice was still bare and the nest looked cold and empty.

Translated by Javaid Qazi

Abdullah Hussein

The Tale of the
Old Fisherman

ABDULLAH HUSSEIN

"This is the place," the old fisherman told them, pointing with his hand.

It was the same place where they had spent that entire day and, before that, many other days. Around an open space with a well in one corner was a brick wall about four feet high. There was just one gate; on the other three sides the entire area was hedged in by tall, multistoried buildings. Known as Jallianwala Garden, it looked more like a cattle yard than a public park. They had spent several days here, recording the statements of journalists and political workers, businessmen and lawyers. Today they happened to run across this old fisherman who, in his eagerness to talk with them, dragged them back to this place, even though they had run out of paper and pencils.

He was short, with small arms and legs, and no one could tell whether nature or age had bent his back. His clothes were in rags and a stench of fish oozed from his body. His face and beard were equally dirty, but an unexpected strength and innocence shone in his eyes. He was one of those men who are born alone and die alone but who, on account of their simplicity and geniality, find frequent occasions to meet and converse with all kinds of people. They looked on as he clambered up the boundary wall like a young boy and perched himself at the top, his feet tucked comfortably beneath him.

"This is the place, my children," he repeated, waving his hand in a circle again.

The shadows were lengthening in the fading light of the sun, and Jallianwala Garden was totally deserted except for them and the two English soldiers on guard with loaded revolvers in their belts. The companions of the ancient, time-scarred hunchback looked at him with eagerness, feeling as though they were standing on the shore of a desolate ocean which had suddenly gone dry and exposed to view all the broken boats and ships that lay on its floor.

Azra, a little apprehensive, leaned against the wall and said, "Tell us everything, fisherman."

"Yes, tell us everything that happened, old fisherman," the others urged.

"All I've done is sell fish, my children, from the first day—since the day I was born—no—since the day I came of age. For at the time I was born, it was my father who would sell fish, while my mother salted them to keep them from rotting. She was a kind and gentle woman. My father used to beat her, and she would beat me, but most of the year we lived together in peace. The beatings occurred only when my father failed to catch any fish. Summer was always the season of trouble and strife, for the rivers would be flooded and the fish would disappear to the bottom of the muddy water and elude our nets. My father would get mad and start cursing the fish and the net and the boat and the heat of the sun, all the time staring at me balefully, seeking some excuse to beat me. But I always managed to stay out of his grasp. I would turn my back on him and continue to paddle in silence, letting his curses fly in and out of my ears. On reaching the bank I would jump out of the boat, run as fast as possible, and soon get out of his range. The rest of the day I would stay away from the house, knowing it would be in turmoil. I would spend the day away from the fishermen's huts, wandering around holes of muddy water, catching and chewing on small fish. During the days of flood I would always carry a piece of salt in my pocket—it's hard to eat raw fish without salt! At first I had some difficulty, but soon it became a habit and I began to relish eating them. They produced a lot of heat and blood in my body. Then in the evening I would return home and peer into the house from the darkness again. I'd stand there outside the door in the dark, nodding with sleep until in utter disgust I would pick up my pet dog and hurl him to the ground. The dog's cries would tell my mother of my return. But she was a clever woman: she would call to me in a sweet voice to come do an errand for her. For instance she'd say, "The dog must be starving, give him his fish." As soon as I stepped in the door she would grab hold of me. Twisting my ears and glaring with fury, she would call me all sorts of names: "Lazy bum! Tramp! Wretch!"—just about all the names that my father called her. Then she would slap my face again and again. At first I used to burst out in real tears; but later, when I grew accustomed to her temper, I would shriek and shout and make so much noise that my father would wake up and curse us both. Yes, those few weeks of flood used to be really bad.

"Once, when the flood continued for a long time and our poverty became terrible and all our dogs died from starvation, my father became irritable. He began to beat me without even bothering to look for an excuse. Becoming desperate, I thought up a plan. One day, when as usual we failed to catch a single fish, my father angrily threw his net down in the bottom of the boat and, cursing the entire world, towered over my head with his fists raised.

"'Listen, Baba,' I said, raising the oar in my hand to defend myself. 'First listen to me.'

"He let his hands fall, but continued to glare at me, sneezing and sputtering in anger. I said, 'If you beat me, I won't row the boat. What will you do then?'

"'I'll row the boat myself,' he said like a madman.

"'And who'll catch the fish?'

"'The fish . . .?' He pulled at his beard in confusion. Then, swearing loudly, he said, 'And just where are there any fish?'

"'But when the flood subsides? Who'll catch them then?'

"He continued to pull thoughtfully at his beard, and then, without a word, sat down on the net. He got my point all right; after that day he never laid a hand on me.

"But, as I said, the days of misfortune used to end eventually. With the advent of winter the snow on the mountains would stop melting and the water in the river would again become clear and the fish would rise close to the surface. Once again we would have a pile of fish, which my mother would clean and salt and pack in gunny bags. We would find some new dogs for pets, my father would regain his good humor, and all through the winter and spring and autumn we would live in peace and comfort like rich and gentle people. And every evening my mother would sit warming her hands in front of the fire and say, 'Lord, thank you very much. It's good that floods come only during the summer and not in winter, for it you don't get fish in winter you're likely to catch pneumonia or rheumatism—not to mention all the cursing and wrangling. Yes, Lord, thank you very much.' She always referred to the beatings she received as 'wrangling.'"

When the old man stopped for breath, the five listeners looked impatient. They had obviously grown tired of the old man's aimless talk.

"Tell us about the firing," they said.

"Wait. . . ." The old man raised a hand to quiet them. "I'll tell you everything. We can sit here until eight in the evening. Let me try to revive my memory. After all these days I have at last found you, people I can talk with. Usually in this city each person is worse than the other. Speak to someone and he remains as dumb as if he had just stepped out of his grave. I have seen many more deaths in epidemics, though . . . But I was speaking of my mother. She was very kind and God-fearing, and also very clever. But she soon died and all her work fell on us. Then we realized her true worth. Now, somehow or other, my father would go alone to catch fish and, whatever catch he would bring, I'd dry in the sun and put in sacks. At night we would sit on the floor facing each other and eat dry fish with chilies. My father, due to his age, never got used to eating uncooked fish; and as long as he lived he suffered because of it. But there was no way out, for neither of us knew how to light a fire and keep it going. It used to make him quite mad to see me eating raw fish with such gusto. 'Son of an animal!' he would shout. 'Son of a crocodile! Look at the way he enjoys them!' And I'd laugh and reply, 'Baba, you call yourself a fisherman but can't eat fish. What kind of a fisherman are you?'

"'I was born from a human being, not an animal,' he would reply. Sometimes I'd add, just to really anger him, 'I can eat a live fish. Can you do the same?'

"'Shut up. You're crazy.'

"'You think so?' I would reply. 'Now look at this.' And with that I'd take a live fish from the pail and put it in my mouth. At the sight of the fish thrashing between my teeth he'd get furious and swing at me with a dried eel. Fearing the cane-like lash of the eel, I'd run outside and stand in the dark listening to his angry mutterings, 'What an age has come upon us! Snakes and pigs are being born in human families. Did you ever hear of such a thing? A live fish—and a live man eating it! One life eating another. . . .' Quietly laughing, I would remain safe in the dark and soon finish the fish."

The old man raised his arms and laughed, showing the three teeth left in his mouth, and as he laughed the wrinkles around his eyes grew thick. Despite their interest in his ramblings, the listeners were getting concerned about the time. They wanted him to stop rambling and come to the real subject.

In the dim light of the fast sinking sun the old man continued.

"But soon we found out what a failure we were at keeping house. The fish that I'd dry and pack in the bags would begin to stink in only two days, and it would become impossible to keep them in the house. They couldn't be sold either, so we would eat as much as we could in two days and throw the rest of the mess in the river. I also noticed that our daily catch was slowly decreasing; and before long we were eating up the daily catch and having nothing left over. Instead of dried fish, my father began to find fresh raw fish more to his liking, for its fat is soft and salty. So as soon as he'd return with the meager catch, he would eat it all up. This won't do at all, I thought. Finally one day, getting tired of my father's stupid ways, I closed the door of the hut and followed him to the river.

"It was the month of Magh . . . or perhaps of Phagun. The snow had not yet melted on the mountains, I remember. The river water was clear all the way to the bottom and one could see the shoals of fish swimming around. I was rowing the boat and my father was standing with his back toward me. I saw that due to age his legs had turned inward and were covered with thick yellow veins. But the day was so beautiful—the color of the river was a deep blue and so was the color of the sky. The wind blew around our heads, and my father's hair, flying in the air, was white as snow and caught the light of the sun. Our boat was rocking gently on the ripples that the wind was making in the river. Then we entered the area where fish were plentiful. The river had cut deep into the bank and looked like a lake. Here we saw thousands of fish of infinite hues, big and small, fat and thin, of all shapes and kinds, with the rays of the sun filtering through the water and playing on their colorful bodies. When my father threw his net, the fish swam away in great consternation but still a lot of big ones got caught. Pulling them into the boat, we turned homeward. I was very happy and was rowing with all my strength when suddenly I saw my father put his hand into the net and pull out a fish from the squirming heap. Holding it in his hand he kept looking at it for some time. It was a very pretty fish—deep blue, with golden spots all over it. It kept opening and closing its gills, staring at God knows what with unblinking eyes.

"'The water is beautiful,' my father said softly. 'My house is ugly. You should go back to your home.' He put his hand in the water and let the fish go. Almost losing my temper, I tried to draw his attention by making loud snuffing noises, but he was lost in his thoughts. Then he picked up another fish. It was purple, with black stripes over the long body, red eyes and a red tail. 'You are beautiful, but my house is ugly. You too should go home,' my father said, and dropped the fish into the water. Striking the water, the fish made a splash with its tail and disappeared. Then my father picked up a third fish, whose skin was white as the whitest silk and which was covered with tiny spots in all the colors of the rainbow. Its head and eyes and lips were also white. My father dropped it too into the water, saying 'You are also beautiful. You too should go home. To fill my belly I need only a few ugly, useless fish.'

"By the time we reached the bank, He had thrown away all the good fish in this manner. I was boiling with rage but kept silent, satisfied that finally I knew the secret behind the daily loss. After we reached the bank I said to him, 'Look here, Baba, starting tomorrow you'll stay at home and I'll go on the boat.'

"'Why?' he shouted angrily.

"'Why?' I shouted back. 'You throw away all the fish, that's why!' I was trembling with rage, and though I was then only eleven, he was frightened by my looks. Bowing his head in silence, he led the way home. After a while he said, 'You'll understand when you too grow old and your woman dies.' I was so furious I didn't bother to answer him.

"After that he remained at home and I went to the river. Once again we managed to store up a lot of fish and once again we began to be considered well-off in that community of fishing folk. But my father was getting older each day, and his sight was weakening. Having spread the fish to dry, he would sit in the shade all day long and advise the fisherman against fighting among themselves, telling those who beat their wives that they ought not to do so or the women would die and then in old age they would have to face the cursed necessity of eating raw fish.

"In this way, by the time I came of age, he was dead."

The old man stopped to catch his breath, laughed and then looked around. His three teeth showed again. By now they were all tired of the old man's rambling loquacity, and Naim had lost all hope of getting any useful details out of him. Only Azra, who had little interest in the work of Naim and his companions, still showed some curiosity.

"Then what happened, old fisherman?" she asked.

"Tell us what happened on the thirteenth of April, fisherman, or else we'll go away," one of the men said.

"All right, all right. I'll tell you everything before eight, my children, don't worry. For at eight you must leave this place; at that time the curfew starts. I was left alone when my father died. Then I began looking around for a woman to take care of the housework, but unfortunately I wasn't very tall, and all the women that I found were taller than me and didn't want me. The one or two who showed some interest turned out to be very ill-tempered, and as you know, my children, I don't like shrews. After some time I gave up the search; I took my father's basket and began to go around selling the daily catch. Now there was no work to do at home, and there was no need for a woman. I started to live happily all by myself and still do, though I left my village and now live in this city. Raw fish and boiled corn are the only things I have ever eaten. I have now lived in this world five years longer than my father did. I have seen many incidents greater than that of the Jallianwala Garden—the mutiny of 1857, when my father had just recently died, and the plague at the turn of the century, and . . . and. . . . But because you are all insisting that I tell you about the Jallianwala incident, I'll talk about that. I can tell you everything that happened on that day and on several days before that.

"You know, some fifty years after the mutiny of 1857, when I told a man all the details of those days, he asked me 'What do you eat?' I said, 'Fish and boiled corn.' 'That's why you're one of the wisest,' he said."

The old man stretched his back and when the listeners caught a glimpse of his three teeth they realized that he was laughing, in his friendly but proud manner.

"The disturbance started on the ninth day of the fourth month, when nine Englishmen were killed in the bazaars of the city. Everything occurred in front of my eyes. They stopped me. There were two of them. I though they wanted to buy my fish. I gladly put my basket on the ground. One of them stayed with me; the other, with a camera to his eye, backed away. Standing at a distance, he took some pictures. Then, taking a silver coin from his pocket, he threw it toward me. His aim was slightly off and I danced and jumped in the air like a crazy man to grab the coin. He took some more pictures. Finally the coin fell on the ground and when I picked it up they were already going away, laughing and talking among themselves. Then, as I was watching, two men attacked them with drawn swords at the corner of the lane. One sword went clean through the stomach of the guy who had taken my pictures; the other stuck in the ribs of his companion. Both of them were dead by the time they hit the dust. I was thunderstruck by the rapidity of the events. Then it occurred to me that only a few moments earlier I had accepted a coin from those foreigners, and it could be that those two swine might try to attack me too. I quickly put that rupee in my inside pocket, picked up my basket, and slipped away. In the next bazaar I saw three more corpses. They lay in the dust a little apart from each other. Their faces still looked warm. They too were foreigners, and their golden hair was dirty with blood and dust. They didn't have cameras. They didn't have anything. Their hands were empty. In the bazaar people were hurriedly closing their shops. A few men stood by the corpses, their faces like children's, pale with fear. Though I felt great pity for those men, I had seen much worse things, so I took the situation in stride, passing by without showing any interest. I didn't even stop my chanting, and kept on calling "Fish for sale, fish for sale." In front of the Darbar Sahib I saw another Englishman. He was dying. A thin dagger had gone through his neck and he was clutching its handle as he suffered his death agony. This was the largest square in the city but was completely deserted, even though it was midday. Nothing alive was in sight. I passed through and continued on my way. But that dying Englishman was very young and very handsome. I couldn't restrain myself from taking a second look at him. At the corner of the street I stopped and looked back. The young man's face was lifted toward the sky in death, and his youthful lips were lifeless. Children, you are fortunate that you are still young and do not know much. I'm an old fisherman. But I have lived a long time and know a few things about life. Young faces, young eyes, young lips—these are the fairest of all things in this world. But when they are made cold. . . . I have seen fish who continue to smile with open eyes even in death. But young men . . . that's a different matter. One feels for a young one. To erase his memory I called loudly 'Fish for sale, fish for sale.' By the time I reached the court buildings I saw three other bodies, lying by the gutters. And beside the corpses I also saw a fire—a silent and hidden fire flaring among the people scurrying in the lane—a fire that burned in their eyes and in their hearts—a terrible wrath that was billowing over the heads of the people. And I tell you the truth, my children; you didn't see it, but I saw it . . . I have seen thousands of dead men and animals and fish; and during the red plague I saw three coffins being carried out of the same door at one time; and I have seen women chanting their laments; and I was present when the trains collided and saw one man's head lying near the neck of another; and I have seen hordes of shouting and bloodthirsty people attacking each other; but never was I frightened, never, for there was nothing to be frightened about in those incidents. But when I saw that silent, suppressed anger raging inside every man and animal and tree of this city, I returned home.

"From that time on, all the business in the city stopped, and military trucks and white soldiers began to make rounds in the streets and bazaars. The people of the city, once scattered over every inch of the ground, now began to collect in small groups in the neighborhood lanes and corners—just like a fishing net, cut in the middle, which begins to collect into small knots. And among these groups there was one which dishonored a white woman in the middle of the bazaar—the incident that was at the root of the later riots. It happened on the third day after the incident. As usual I was making my rounds, carrying the fish basket. I was feeling rather upset, for by that time the fish had started to smell and there was nothing but hatred in my heart for them. I had stopped shouting my wares—after so many days there was nothing left in them to tout—but I was hoping that some kindhearted person fond of fish might relieve me of them. When I reached the lane that connects the big market with the vegetable market, I was stopped in my tracks. A white woman came running out of the lane and behind her came a baying mob. They caught her in the center of the market and stood around glaring at her with hate in their eyes. The woman's hair was dusty and her legs were covered with mud. She stood in the middle of that mob, turning slowly on her heels like a mechanical doll, and her face was as colorless as white fish. For some moments those men kept staring at her in sullen silence. Then one of them stepped out, grabbed the collar of her dress, and tore it down to her knees. She screamed and that broke the spell. The pack fell upon her. Right in front of my eyes they kept snatching at her like crows and vultures. I must say though, she was a terrific woman; indeed she was. Quite remarkable. The moment she got a chance she jumped out form under those men and started running. There was nothing left now of her flowery dress, and only a little piece of underclothing covered her buttocks and hung over her breasts. Her hair was dishevelled and she ran like a witch, straining her legs. I can still picture her well-rounded buttocks and heavy thighs. Ah. . . . It occurred to me then that if that woman were sitting at my house eating fish, she would look very pleasing. Ah. . . . As she disappeared down an alley, with that mob close behind her, I returned home cursing the bastards.

"That night, for the first time in my life, I couldn't go to sleep. I usually sleep well, for sleep is essential for good health, but that night I just couldn't. I felt parched, as if there was no moisture left in my body. I began to think of my health. I tried heating the room by lighting a fire. Then I got worried about the leftover fish and decided to spread them out against the wall to dry. I lay down on my mat in the corner, but I still felt wide awake. Thinking perhaps it was because of the stink of the fish, I got up again and, gathering the fish in a heap, covered them with my basket. Then I lay down on my right side, since that's the way I usually sleep; but it didn't help. So I dragged my mat close to the fire, a foolish thing to do, for I was already roasting. I got up and was kneeling on the floor, wondering about my condition, when a thought suddenly occurred to me. I removed the basket and selected a rotting fish.

"'I can't seem to find any sleep tonight. So let's have a little chat,' I said. The fish remained silent, though her mouth was wide open. 'If my father were alive, he'd have let you go before you died. But I don't do such crazy things. So open your ears wide and listen to what I tell you. Don't laugh, for your kids and other relatives may be crying over your death even now.' The fish kept her mouth open in a wide smirk which infuriated me. 'So you find it funny? You died long ago, you beast, but your dull eyes are still open. You don't sleep yourself, and you won't let anyone else sleep. Here. . . .' and I threw her in the fire. Soon she was crackling and sputtering in the flames; but her eyes were still open and the smirk was still on her face. In my anger I thew another fish into the fire; her eyes were open too but she looked more sober. The smell of burning fish soon filled the room, and you know, my children, how that smell can make your mouth water. But it was past midnight and I didn't feel like eating anything, so I ignored the idea and selected another fish from the heap. 'Your skin is so soft and pretty; you might be able to find a customer. You better stay.' And I put her aside. This game seemed to help. So after talking awhile with those fish, and burning a few of them in the fire, I fell asleep.

"When I awoke in the morning the sun was already fairly high and people were up and around. But though the streets sounded alive again after so many days of silence, I felt a strange apprehension. Rubbing my eyes to see better, I stepped outside. People seemed to be in a great hurry, and they were all going in the same direction, as though they were headed for some fish auction which had already begun and each of them was eager to buy the best lot. But one thing marked them as different from buyers of fish, and that was their silence. No one seemed to speak to anyone else although among them there were both old and young, big and small, fat and thin. What amazed me more were the looks on their pale faces as they hurried by me with clenched teeth and unseeing eyes. It frightened me and yet aroused my curiosity; I quickly filled my basket and joined them. No one paid any attention to me, so I clenched my teeth like the rest of them and began to walk with my chest thrown forward. Everywhere one looked, lines of people were rushing in the same direction. When we reached the market square we saw a number of white soldiers standing fully armed. As we moved into the square, they took up positions as if in a war and loaded their guns. Then a squad of Indian policemen arrived. They had bamboo poles in their hands and began to beat us with them. Some of us were badly hit and some were not, but we were all pushed out of the square. One stick hit my basket, which fell to the ground, scattering all the fish in the dirt. Trying to retrieve them I was hit a few times on the back, but I didn't give up, and managed to collect most of them. Suddenly loud shouts and slogans filled the air; another crowd had come from the opposite direction and was trying to enter the square. But the police squad stopped them too, and soon they came around and joined us. With their arrival our quiet mob became vocal and began to shout similar slogans. When the noise became unbearable we started marching toward this place where we are now. I was surrounded by people who pushed and fell and shouted, their faces free of any fear and lit instead with passion and anger. Their shouts seemed to make the sky tremble.

We kept marching like that, shouting and rushing down the streets and alleys. Lots of small crowds came and joined us on the way, and the few soldiers who tried to stop us were pushed aside.

"When we entered this park it looked like an ocean without a shore. It was already quite full before our arrival, and wave after wave of people kept coming after us, jamming into the park. Under a thick cloud of dust raised by their feet, hundreds of thousands of people were milling around as though it were the day of judgement, and it was impossible to stay in any one spot. The dust filled my nostrils, my feet were crushed a million times, and torrents of sweat ran down my body though it was still spring. I was cursing the mob, and my own foolishness, but it was impossible to get out of there. I was also feeling very embarrassed at being the only one with a basket on my head. Just then I noticed a small boy, hardly twelve, who was crying and seemed lost. Feeling sorry for the poor kid, I took him by the hand and drew him to one side. He kept crying, so I looked into my basket, selected a good-looking fish, and gave it to him. He then became quiet and was soon quite happy playing with the fish, so I told myself that my bringing the basket had done some good after all.

"As the people kept pouring in, the roar of their slogans grew louder and louder. The Muslims were shouting the names of Allah and their religious leaders, while the Hindus and Sikhs were shouting their own sacred slogans. Then I turned around and saw a dark bearded man standing on high ground, waving his hand to quiet the crowd. But his wild gestures and flying beard seemed to have little effect on the mob. As I watched, a white man dressed like an army officer came up behind him. He shoved the bearded man off the stand and began to shout something to the crowd, threatening with his hands. There was a brief moment of silence when we could all hear his angry voice, and, though it was impossible to understand what he was saying, his gestures and the expression on his face made it clear that he wanted us to get the hell out of there. Suddenly a roar rose from the crowd and someone threw a shoe in his direction. Then more shoes came flying toward him from all sides, looking like flocks of geese rising from the surface of a lake. The people who were near the army officer stood there in silent terror, and most of the shoes fell on them. I kept my wits and held on to my shoes, for you know, my children, I only have one pair. When the shoes were gone, people began taking off their clothes. Now turbans and shirts and undershirts were being rolled into balls and thrown at the officer. Soon about half the people were partly naked, and a few were so shameless they took off everything and ran around completely nude. But soon there was nothing more to throw; only the tumult and noise continued, in which the mob and the army officer both took part. Then someone noticed my basket, and before I could step back, a score of hands reached forward and pulled it out of my grasp. Some of the men glared at me with bloodthirsty eyes when they saw the fish. Then they picked them up and threw them with all their strength toward the white man. The fish that landed short were picked up by the men at that spot and thrown forward, and then farther and farther until one fish hit the army officer right between his eyes. He caught it as it slithered down his face and looked at it in disbelief. Then raising his head, he looked at the crowd, then at the fish again, then back at the crowd, and suddenly with a jerk he smashed the fish in the face of the man standing in front of him. Next he threw his arms in the air, shouting like a maniac, and then suddenly the firing began.

"In a man's lifetime, he's seldom likely to see a scene like the one that followed. People were running in mad confusion like fish caught in a net; but the pursuing bullets were faster than the fleeing men. . . . There was one man who was running with a hand over my shoulder when he was hit. He jumped into the air like an acrobat and was held there for a moment by another bullet, and then another bullet, until he turned a somersault; and when he hit the ground he was already dead, though his face had lost none of its passion. His body was soon hidden by other bodies. In my panic I kept running even when I saw my ancestral basket rolling on the ground as bullets kept hitting it. Then suddenly my feet went cold and a shriek escaped my lips, for in front of me was that well . . . that dry well . . . do you see it over there? . . . that same one. It was only a few yards away from where I had stopped. Some people running by me had fallen into it, then many more people, and soon the well was so filled with dead and the dying that the fleeing men could run over the human bodies. Running along crouched under the pursuing bullets, I passed the spot where we are sitting now. You see this wall? It's empty now, but at that time human bodies were hanging over its entire length. Their legs were on the inside but their arms hung over the other side with bellies resting on the wall. These were the people who had tried to escape over the wall, thinking it was low enough, but as they reached the top they were hit by the bullets. And as I stared at them from inside the park they looked like pieces of laundry strung out by some washerwoman to dry in the sun. Did you notice these holes in the wall? Ah. . . . You who go around asking people for the news, what do you know! You can never know the punishment that was given to this ill-fated city! Ah . . .

"As I came out I saw some dogs pulling at a fish. It was that fat white fish I had put aside the night before in the hope of finding a good buyer. Now, as I saw these strange 'buyers,' I felt like laughing, but it was no time for laughter. I had to get away from there as quickly as possible to save my life.

"Stumbling and falling, I finally reached the spot where they had attacked that white woman the day before. The escaping people had been stopped at the mouth of the street, and after much pushing and pulling, when I reached the front, I saw the strangest sight. On both sides of the street white soldiers stood ready to shoot, and a river of human bodies seemed to be flowing through the middle. These were men like you and me lying on the ground and crossing that twenty-five yard stretch on their bellies. They were not allowed to use their knees or elbows. They were told—all of us were told—to crawl like snakes, for at that spot we had behaved like snakes toward their white woman. Anyone who tried to raise himself on his knees or elbows was immediately shot. Then the soldiers thought up something even better: they lined up on one side of the market and began to shoot just six inches above the heads of the crawling people. The slithering cowards buried their faces in the ground and inched forward with the help of only their toes and nails. In the meantime wave after wave of fleeing people kept coming, for this was the only route of escape from the park. As soon as a place became free, someone from the crowd would fall on his face and begin crawling in the dirt. As you know, my children, crawling is not very difficult for us fisherman. My father, may God bless him with peace, had taught me when I was only six to float on the surface of the water without moving a limb. So when my turn came I had to drag my head on the ground which injured the side of my skull so that it remained swollen for many days. I went across with greater agility than most men, however. There was one old man crawling along side of me, with not a single hair on his head; his skull was bleeding and one cheek dragged a wide line behind him in the dirt. This old man was crying bitterly, though he was also somewhat ashamed of his tears. At the end of the passage, when we got up to run, I recognized him. He used to buy fish from me every Thursday and had three grown-up sons and a large grocery store.

"For many days after that I stayed away from that place, but from a distance I saw people being forced to crawl over that stretch of ground—though crawling is unbecoming to human beings. I never recovered my ancestral basket.

"Now you'd better leave this place, my children. The curfew will be starting any moment and then for twelve hours anyone found in this area will be shot at sight. I've tried your patience a lot, I know, but you yourselves asked me to tell you everything. 'Old man, tell us everything.' So I've told you every bit of it. . . . But you don't need to be dismayed, my children, for I have seen worse things."

"Aren't you going to leave this place?" one listener asked.

"No."

"Are you a Muslim or a Hindu?" Naim asked quickly.

"Aha, that's a nice one." The old hunchback gestured with his index finger and laughed. "Yes, that's a nice question. Frankly, I don't know. You see . . . well, I was too busy to ask my father, and my father was too busy to tell me. The fisherman only knows how to toil; he doesn't have time for such questions." Then he pointed toward the white soldiers. "I've also told them everything. They don't bother me any more. They know I'm not interested in those things. I'm only an old fisherman, somewhat hunchbacked."

On their way back they kept turning their heads to look at that small dark figure who, tired after the long discourse, now sat quiet and alone on the wall, while a desolate night spread around him. The barrier of night gradually thickened until he disappeared from sight. But for many years after that evening, that dark and lonely figure kept coming back before their eyes.

Translated by C.M. Naim and Gordon Roadarmel

Note: This chapter from Abdullah Hussein's award-winning novel Udās Naslēn *(Sad Generations) harks back to a tragic and shameless episode from the British colonial rule in India. Following the enactment of Rowlatt Acts in India, M.K. Gandhi launched a movement of protest with public meetings and strikes. In the Punjab, which had just witnessed the third Afghan war, passions rose to a*

feverish pitch and the otherwise peaceful protests became violent. Four Europeans were mob-murdered at Amritsar on 10 April 1919. The British retaliation was swift and exceptionally harsh: three days later, the British, without prior notice or warning, sent troops under the command of General Dyer, who broke up a meeting of 10,000 people in a large enclosed area known as the Jallianwala Bagh. According to official estimate, casualties included 379 Indians killed and 1,200 wounded. The massacre was followed by imposition of martial law and a number of most humiliating punitive orders. Krishan Chandar, an ardent nationalist writer, has graphically captured the event in his short story, "Amritsar," in two parts, "Before Independence" and "After Independence" (for which, see his Ham vahshī hēṅ *([Lucknow: Kitābī Dunyā, 1947 or 1948]). The event can also be seen in all its gory detail in the recent film "Gandhi."*
—Editor.

Iqbal Majeed

Two Men, Slightly Wet

IQBAL MAJEED

The rain started quite suddenly. The fat drops came down with such force that they hurt. No one had thought it would rain. It wasn't the season and the weather hadn't been changing. When a big change occurs unexpectedly we are at first merely startled, then find our lives totally disturbed. In just a short time the rain turned everything topsy-turvy. People had come out without raincoats or umbrellas, now they scurried around seeking shelter.

I am not different from others. I too was momentarily stunned when the first raindrops hit me. But the next moment I decided to do what the others had done. I was walking down the road; I ran and took shelter under the first roof I could find. I was still trying to catch my breath after the sudden dash when another man came staggering in. We glanced at each other once, then continued with our efforts to compose ourselves. I wiped my face with my handkerchief, looked over my shirt and pants then began to watch the road.

"Now who could have known it would rain!" the other man remarked, perhaps to get my response. But I was in no mood to start anything, I remained silent. Nothing got started.

I had thought that the shower, being unusual for the season, would peter out in a few minutes, but a glance at the sky killed that hope. I couldn't understand how so many clouds had gathered overhead without anyone noticing. By now it was really pouring. The dark clouds covered the entire sky. The road in front of me, crowded a moment ago, was filled instead with water. I was still reviewing these matters when I was startled to feel some cold drops fall on my shoulders. For the first time I noticed that it was a roof above our heads and not the sky.

I guess something similar happened to the other man. Simultaneously we glanced at each other again, then together our eyes turned upward.

Where we had taken shelter was a broken-down porch, jutting out in front of the main door of a rather old house. It was barely five feet square. The door behind us was bolted and locked. The termite-eaten beams of the old-fashioned roof sagged; they now glistened with the water that was seeping in. Slowly the moisture would accumulate into drops, which would fatten and, unable to hold their weight, fall like ripe mangos. Suddenly the wind brutally turned in our direction and one water-laden gust left us drenched to our knees. I stepped back, furious. The other man seemed almost to jump. There was really no space in the back, but he struggled as if the wall itself would move back against his onslaught. The wind receded, but increasingly drops of water kept falling down on us from the beams and from the cracks in the ceiling. My companion had now started to twist and turn, as if trying to shrink into himself.

I glanced at the wide road. Once in a while some car would go splashing by, its windows rolled up. One or two men went by on bicycles, grim faced, drenched to the skin, furiously pedaling away. I liked the attitude of those bicycle-riders, but the rest bored me. I looked toward my companion. He was dressed in a long shirt and pajamas; the shirt was wet at the shoulders. The drops from the ceiling had not left his back dry, his arms either. The pajamas, of course, had already been taken care of by that big gust a moment ago. Seeing the condition he was in, I surveyed my own clothes. It was obvious we were in the same mess. I could barely suppress my anger.

"Well, it doesn't look like it will stop," I remarked, shifting my pose and looking at my companion as if I wished to be forgiven for my previous indifference.

"Yes, the clouds mean business."

"And this place doesn't look very safe either," I said, glancing at the ceiling.

He too looked up. Then our eyes met again, briefly. Frankly, I was feeling a bit peeved; I now wished to get away from that place. I could see a man or two making slow progress on the road. While I was struggling to decide, a few more drops fell on my head. I quickly shifted to another spot. But now the entire ceiling was leaking; the drops of water followed me whichever way I tried to shrink. The same thing was happening to the other man; he too was constantly moving from one spot to another. Finally, in exasperation, I turned to him.

"Come, let's get out of here."

He looked at me and quietly smiled, but then merely shrank into another corner. Perhaps my remark struck him as too silly to deserve any attention.

But I was enraged. It was suffocating under the porch. The drops dripping from the beams pierced through my clothes. The unpaved floor was now all mud, and in a few depressions water had formed puddles. I looked at my companion with some intensity, but his face showed no sign of boredom or anxiety. I kept looking at him, expecting him to change his mind any moment, but I was disappointed. He stubbornly remained where he was, as he was. I could no longer control myself; this time I addressed him irately.

"You think you can save yourself from getting drenched by standing here?"

"Seems rather doubtful," he replied without enthusiasm.

"Do you think this rain will stop in the next ten minutes?"

"It doesn't look like it," he replied, stressing every word.

"Then why put up with this misery?" I said with some heat. "If we must get drenched, why here, so abjectly?"

"Let's wait a bit more, it may stop," he said, shifting his position, and began to wipe his face with the hem of his shirt, now clinging to his body like a second skin.

I drew in a deep breath, then exhaled, to relieve some of that suffocating feeling, then turned to watch the road. No change had occurred in the rain; it still came down in torrents. In anguish I looked to the left and to the right once again. No other shelter was close enough. There was a gas station, but quite far away, and beyond that the compound-wall of a house. I knew that house. A lady doctor lived there, and its gate had a big sign, "Beware of Dog." I was still stretching my neck, trying to peer through the sheets of rain, when a dog came panting onto the porch, and flapped its ears. It was immediately shooed off by both of us.

"Look, it's silly to stand here like this," I addressed my companion once again.

"What should we do then?" he asked.

"Let's get out of here."

"But the rain is pretty bad."

"So what?" I said, flaring up. "We are already dripping from head to toe. Don't tell me you still think you're protected by this roof?"

"But . . . still . . . ," he stopped short.

"Well, I won't stay here a minute longer. I'm leaving."

"As you wish." He tried to shrink further into himself.

I was secretly burnt up by his reply. I had thought there was much in common between him and me. Going out of the house. Getting suddenly caught in the rain. Taking shelter under a roof that was veined with cracks. Getting drenched in that miserable manner. With so much in common, I had expected our thoughts would also be the same. But I could make no sense of the stupid way he was behaving.

Pushing out my chest I lifted one foot off the ground and began to roll up the leg of my wet pants. I was perturbed. I was angry. The discovery that my assumptions had been wrong had left me with a bitter feeling. There was so much difference in the way we thought! Our paths were far apart! Even our notions of gain and loss didn't coincide. He wanted to get wet little by little, standing under a leaky roof. His entire body would get drenched; the roof would not give him respite. It would continue to rain drops on him. And the drops would fall on his hair, roll down the back of his neck, down his back, to the tip of his spine. No doubt the process was slow, it needed time, but he was not such a fool that he didn't know what the result was going to be. Then why was he clinging to this porch? Perhaps he had persuaded himself to be satisfied with what he had managed to get at his very first attempt?

Lazy!

Stupid!

Coward! Dead!

I spat on the ground and, pushing back my shoulders, swaggered out into the torrent. I didn't look back once. Gusts of wind and sheets of rain welcomed me.

Struggle! Explore! Search! That is life.

I belong to the new generation. I think differently. That roof was leaking and he was getting more and more wet. To stand in wet clothes, exposed to the wind, was very dangerous. He could catch cold. Sorry, but each of us would rather die his own way. We make our own selections. Not everyone wants to die of cancer, just as not everyone prefers to jump under a train. But if that man was to catch cold and die of double pneumonia, just imagine what the gossips would say:

Fool! Stood under a leaky roof all day long hoping that the rain would stop!

Such is the end of all wretched, useless people. It all depends on the way we think, the way we look at life. We all die. And how we die, that is also insignificant. Good, we can have a good talk on this subject. It is a good topic. I will go to the coffee house and stand there under a fan. My shirt and pants are made of Terylene, they will dry in a few minutes. Then I will ask my companions there, what they would like to die for. How they die, that is their business. I only want to know the goal for which they can accept death. To catch pneumonia under a leaky roof and die, is that a great goal? I know they will listen to me. They will say, "In you speaks the new awareness of the Sixties." I shall answer, "You are right, that is the big difference, the way we think." And then I will tell them more. That there is still a man standing on that porch; he doesn't want to get wet under the heavens, nevertheless he is getting drenched. He has not come with me. But I did choose to walk and get drenched under the wide sky. The clouds burst over me, but my body withstood their onslaught. It is only now that I have reached the comfortable seat and the solid roof of the coffee house. I have explored and asserted. Suffered the buffets of rain in this pursuit. I was not scorned by the rain; I felt attached to it.

Attached! . . . They will sit up at this word.

That the attacking gusts of wind and water aroused in me amazement, inspired me to seek.

Amazement! . . . To seek!

And after my companions carefully take hold of these words I will tell them that there was this very strong belief within me that attaching myself to that rain and moving with it I would definitely reach a new and better state.

Belief! . . . They will quickly take possession of that word too. Afterwards, completely forgetting that man caught in the rain, they will bring out slowly, like misers, the four words they had grabbed from me.

Attachment, curiosity and wonder, and belief.

Then their eyelids will droop and shift, like a parrot's, and in soft tones they will inform me that in the Rigvedic age man in fact had these four great things:

Attachment, wonder and curiosity, and belief.

We have none, and that is the problem. None of us can write a veda, any veda. . . . But what was it that I was saying about that man caught in the rain?

But the rain. . . .

Suddenly I realized the rain had stopped. My thoughts began to sag. I looked up at the sky; the clouds were fleeing. The coffee house was still pretty far away. Without my willing it so my feet were making rapid, but bumpy, progress on the long rain-washed road. My pants and shirt clung to my body; the lines of the undershirt could clearly be seen. I recalled there was still one cigarette in the packet of Char Minar in my pocket. I took the packet out and glanced around. A bit ahead there was a roadside tea shop; its stove seemed full of glowing coals, fanned by the wind. The wind was quite chilly.

Stopping outside by the blazing stove I took out the cigarette. It was wet through. Putting it to my lips, I first shook off some of the water from my clothes, then borrowing a match from the vendor, lit the cigarette. But I could get only a couple of puffs. It sort of dissolved into pieces; only a whole lot of tobacco crumbs were left sticking to my lips. Spitting them out furiously I asked the vendor for a cup of tea, and moved closer to the coals to dry myself. The road was again full of passersby.

"So now you're drying your clothes here!" someone said by my side.

I looked up. That same stranger was going into the tea shop, his face wide with laughter.

"Come, have a cup of tea," he called to me after he sat down at a table. I went over and sat down beside him. The wind was still gusty. My clothes felt a bit drier.

"You were in too much of a hurry, for the rain stopped only ten minutes after you left," he remarked while squeezing water out of the hem of his shirt.

I looked at him without much enthusiasm and mumbled, "And if it hadn't stopped?"

"Then there was no choice."

I felt sorry at his answer. To misuse precious words is as saddening as using a bullet to kill a tiny bird.

"You are a common man," I retorted.

"Oh? And how is that?"

"The same way as all the other common people."

He wasn't a bit put off by my remark; he merely laughed. When the tea arrived he began to stir his cup with gusto.

"I would like to tell you in all seriousness that you, and all people like you, are a handicap to themselves."

Instead of appearing hurt at my remark, he gave a short laugh and looking straight into my eyes, said, "I guess you're angry because I didn't keep you company."

"Don't be silly," I said heatedly. "Who needed your company? I wasn't Napoleon going off to some battle and in need of followers. I had merely made a simple observation."

"What observation?"

"That if you were already getting wet why not move on in the rain. I ask you now, did you succeed in staying dry?"

Instead of a reply he intently looked for a moment at my shirt and then asked with a smile, "This fabric is called polyester, isn't it?"

"Yes. But it can also get wet." I tried to be sarcastic.

"Your pants are of the same fabric perhaps?" He scrutinized my pants.

"Yes."

"There isn't any pocket in your shirt, is there?"

"No, there isn't."

He remained silent for a while and finished the tea, then said, "I know I have no right to ask you this, but if it is all right with you tell me if you have anything else on you?"

"What do you mean?"

"I mean do you have anything in your pants' pockets?"

"I have got some change."

"Any paper money?"

"No."

"Any picture . . . that you wish to carry with you?"

"No."

"Any letter or document that you consider precious and want to protect?"

"No."

"Any medicine? I mean pills or capsules that you may be carrying to give to someone seriously ill and waiting for them?"

"No, I have nothing of that sort on me."

"Perhaps some talisman on which you rely and which is expected to bring you success so long as you carry it on you?"

"Now what sort of nonsense is that?"

"That means you don't carry a talisman?"

"No, I do not."

"That means you have on this time only pants, a shirt, a pair of shoes and some change?"

"That's right."

"And your shirt will dry sooner than mine?"

"True."

"Likewise your pants will dry quicker than mine?"

"Indeed."

"Well, there it is."

He began to smile.

"What?" I asked, incensed.

"You have nothing else on you but your clothes, your shoes and some change, but I do. The things that you have, it won't matter at all if they got wet—but even if my clothes and shoes get soaked I want to protect that one thing."

"What thing?" I shouted.

"The thing that I have and you don't."

"Well, what is it?" I was quite angry now. "Stop trying to trap me like some smarty lawyer. Nothing is that important in the world. You are only talking rubbish."

He didn't reply immediately. Leisurely he counted out the money to the vendor; after we had both come out of the shop, he patted me on the shoulder and said, "When you will have something in your pocket that you may badly want to protect you too will prefer to get soaked under a roof rather than outside. At that time that will be your handicap." Then he walked away.

My polyester clothes were now completely dry.

Translated by C.M. Naim

Hasan Manzar

The Poor Dears

HASAN MANZAR

A cold, wet wind was blowing outside as my plane landed at Heathrow Airport. In the terminal building I spotted Cathy in the crowd coming to receive their relatives and felt reassured. I was no longer worried about how I would get to my flat.

I dumped my baggage in the trunk of Cathy's white Ford and flopped down beside her on the seat. After she pulled the car out of the airport traffic into a calmer street, I lit a cigar and said, "Open the window a crack, or you'll wind up dead behind the wheel in your quiet, cozy world."

"You may keep smoking," she said, without taking her eyes off the road.

I closed my eyes and dozed off. I awakened only when I felt Cathy's hand trying to remove the cigar butt from between my lips.

"How did you know I was asleep?" I asked.

"How? You snore."

We had reached my flat. Standing on the dark, cobbled street, I thanked Cathy, promising to tell her about my travels in the morning, and said goodbye to her. Then I looked around impassively. Empty milk bottles stood outside doors in the dim, grey light. Except for one, all the other flats were dark behind closed curtains.

The same old place. I was home for certain! It is a rare virtue in Cathy that she never asks questions unless I am in a mood to answer them.

In the morning I went through my mail. There were bills, bank statements—the usual stuff.

The cleaning lady came and started work. At one point she asked, "How did your trip go, Mr. Hasan?"

"It went quite well, thank you," I said, offering her the red box of Benson & Hedges.

She thanked me and took out a cigarette. As she put it carefully away in her apron pocket, she said, "I mustn't waste such an expensive cigarette. I'll smoke after I'm done with cleaning."

I gave her the whole box and said, "Come on, old girl, have a smoke with me first. You can work later."

"So you felt quite at home there, Mr. Hasan?" she asked puffing a cloud of smoke.

I told her that if by "there" she meant India and Pakistan, then she was mistaken. I hardly even knew the names of my relatives in those places. Or if she meant some other countries, then, until a few months ago, I knew no more about them than did an ordinary Londoner.

I scarcely remember when the cleaning lady left and when Cathy walked in. She had come to take down my travel notes, which she would then type and return to me properly arranged, so that I could start work on my new book. A number of trifling chores which, like any ordinary traveller, I had foisted upon myself, kept getting in the way, however. I wanted to get them out of the way. For instance, the decrepit old man I had run into at the Angkor Wat ruins, the grand temple dedicated to Lord Vishnu, had asked me through a bout of nasty coughing, "I hear that in England they have come up with a brand new drug for curing bronchial asthma?"

Nearly exhausted from my strolls through the myriad pathways and balconies of the temple that sprawled over some 500 acres, I had just sat down, removed my burning feet from my shoes and plunged them into the cool, refreshing dirt. The old man sat close by, carefully holding my movie and still cameras in his lap to protect them from the dust. In my tranquil surroundings, I began to make notes.

The sky was crowded with dark, low-hanging rain clouds. The old man panted for breath. "I hear," he said, as if to himself, "*that* drug roots out the disease."

So, I jotted down the old man's name and address in my notes on the Angkor Wat ruins, setting them apart carefully within parentheses. Even as I did that, I couldn't suppress a smile thinking how Cathy would type out the lines on a separate sheet of paper which she would then hand over to me saying, "Perhaps this gentleman belongs to the present century; we can't possibly include his name and address in the book."

I promised the old man to ask my doctor friends back in England about the drug. If such a drug really existed, I would be sure to send it to him. One of my journalist friends could bring enough quantities of it to last him six to twelve months.

I had been expecting my offer to brighten up the old man—amazing, isn't it, how the East eagerly awaits every new discovery or invention to come from the West!—but his face remained entirely expressionless. With measured politeness, he said, "All right, sir, if you say so."

The old man handed me back my cameras and got busy in his work. He had as little hope of hearing from me again as he had of being able to fall asleep that night; and failure to get the drug would have hurt him as little, I thought, as the realization that his life was coming to an end. He would have accepted them both with the ascetic detachment befitting a Buddhist monk. "Time" and "human dependence" had become meaningless words for him in the ruins of that centuries-old temple which resembled a veritable town in its vast sweep.

Then there was this other *bhikshu* I had met in a Buddhist monastery in Sri Lanka. I had mentioned to him a recent publication from New York and London which contained color pictures of all the important Buddhist monuments the world over.

This monastery, flanked on all sides by king coconut palms, was a short distance from Colombo. I was visiting it for the second time. I had first come here when I was on my way to Kandy and Anuradhapura, and now again as I was leaving Sri Lanka for India. In between, I had managed a trip to the ruins of Anuradhapura and taken pictures of the brick *maths* erected during the Sinhalese period in honor of Buddha.

The Temple of Buddha's Tooth at Kandy, with its every stone, wooden beam and the delicate art carved on them, was also fresh in my memory. I was terribly disappointed that they would not open for me the room which housed the celebrated relic, so that I could verify for myself whether there really was a tooth or whether the gullible people had just placed their faith in a velvet box.

The ceiling of the balcony outside this room held a painting of an elephant. I would have passed through the balcony almost without noticing it, or would have at most given it a cursory glance, had not one of the temple devotees invited me to look at it carefully. I looked up without enthusiasm, hoping to find a profile of Ganesh, the Elephant God, but stopped short. The devotee let out a short, gentle, experienced laugh. The accomplished painter had so skillfully depicted a bevy of young female devotees of the shrine, that they merged into the figure of a colossal elephant. I asked him about the painter but he chose to ignore my question, thinking, perhaps, that it was insignificant. Instead, he started telling me about some white flowers that lay in front of the statue of a seated Buddha.

I asked the same question of my bhikshu friend in Colombo during my second meeting with him. The intervening period, which I had spent in different cities of Sri Lanka, had created a sort of closeness between us—closeness which was obvious from his expression but which he was loath to admit. I guess this was because intimacy bred the very attachment which he had wanted to curb by renouncing the world and adopting the austere, saffron-dyed garb of a bhikshu. My single question prompted him to ask a few of his own about India, about Burma. Finally, I gulped down the coconut milk he had offered and got up.

It was to him that I had promised to send the book. I telephoned Foyles. They did have it in stock; price: 2 pounds. I placed the order and instructed them to send it directly to the monk in Sri Lanka. This done, I crossed his name off my check list. I felt a sense of relief slowly coming over me—I couldn't have wanted it more.

A little while later Faiq Ali telephoned from Manchester. He wanted to know about his relatives whom I had met in Karachi. It was strange, wasn't it, that before embarking on my voyage to the East it was I who had asked him, "Well, aren't you going to give me the addresses of all those first and second cousins you keep telling me about all the time?" and now it was he who was so impatient to find out from me about those same "first" and "second" cousins: "What kind of people are they? Did they treat you well?" so on and so forth, as if Naima and her relatives were in fact mine, not his.

The only reason I had asked Faiq for addresses was that I wanted to see firsthand how people lived in Pakistan, what sort of problems they had, what kind of hopes, and dreams they cherished. One rarely gets an accurate idea of a country and its people by staying up in hotels, or reaching out to them through tourist guides and travel books.

The morning after I arrived in Karachi from Colombo I first confirmed my reservations in hotels where I was to stay during my visit to different cities in West Pakistan, then made a few phone calls regarding my schedule. Finally, I called the European drug manufacturing company where Naima worked. I had thought everybody would know her there. This was not the case. I was told that she was just a packing girl, free to talk on the phone only during the lunch hour. I had not finished talking when the receptionist rudely hung up. I dialed again, this time asking to speak with the General Manager of the company. The man at the other end sounded irritated. Why didn't I go to Naima's house and ask her whatever important thing it was that I wanted to ask her? Why was I wasting his time? But when I told him that I was a writer from England on a trip to Pakistan and knew next to nothing about this country, his voice changed noticeably. He asked me courteously for my phone number and instructed someone on the intercom in Urdu, "Look, there is some girl called Naima who works in the packing department. Ask her to come right away to my office and take the phone." He then politely asked me to wait awhile.

As I waited I could hear faint snatches of some Pakistani music playing in his office and two men talking in one of the regional languages.

When I picked up the phone again I heard the voice of a frightened female at the other end talking in barely audible tones. This was Naima who, I sensed, was quite embarrassed talking to a perfect stranger like myself in the inhibiting presence of her boss, scared that her voice might ruin the decor of his room. I guessed from her voice that she must have been around twenty years old.

"What do you want?" she asked in a whisper.

The rest was more or less a monologue. Had it not been for her faint "Yeses" that echoed dimly through the receiver from time to time, I would have thought the line had been disconnected, all the more so as the sound of Pakistani music had meanwhile died out and the other human voices, too, had stopped.

As I talked to her I couldn't resist imagining a frightfully pretty girl at the other end—all alone, skewered by the lustful stares of the men in the room, trying her best to crawl into the receiver to avoid those piercing glances, but who did not know how. Even her "yeses" were no longer audible to me.

I told her that I was a friend of her cousin Faiq and had come to spend a few days in Karachi. Then I asked her if I could, perhaps, come and visit her at her house. I asked her for her address and mentioned that I would drop by some evening after my return from Taxila.

"Tell me the day you want to come and give me your address," she whispered. "I will have my brother come and pick you up."

This was the second and the last full sentence the girl uttered. I fished through my datebook and gave her the date on which I was scheduled to leave for Beirut and my address.

I related the details of my meeting with Naima and her folks to Faiq. All he seemed to be interested in, though, was my comment that if he was looking for an Eastern wife he would not find a better girl than Naima from east of Suez to Cambodia.

To return to my meeting with Naima and her family. On the appointed day, the hotel receptionist sent to my room a youth whose face was all but covered with pock marks. He looked just as frightened as Naima had sounded over the phone. He had come to escort me to their house. I offered him some refreshments but he declined, adding courteously, "Back home, we are all waiting for you to join us for tea."

The poor boy seemed over-awed by the hotel more than by me. It was probably the first time that he had set foot in it, and was feeling quite out of place in its plush, swank environment. I asked the waiter for a taxi and came out of the hotel with the youth.

Throughout the ride I remained silent. I didn't wish to embarrass my young companion further. He, on his part, preoccupied himself with giving directions to the cab driver. We passed through different parts of the city, each with its peculiar lifestyle. The faces, bodies and garb of most of the pedestrians suggested that we were proceeding from affluence to poverty, from a world of plenty to a world of dire need. The women in Naima's neighborhood flitted about in veils. Children, some barefooted, some with runny noses, romped around. Here and there along the street some people had set up cots on which they sat or lay. There were no foreigners.

Naima's brother led me into a dull, pale building. We climbed several flights of dark, dank stairs and entered a flat on the third floor. I had to spend some time alone in the living room. In fact, I had expected that and was mentally prepared for it. As I sat there waiting for my hosts to appear, I realized my mistake. I should have met these people immediately after my arrival in Pakistan, so that on a second visit around the time of my departure we would have become informal enough for me to gauge their true feelings, and to have some idea of their hopes and aspirations. It is amazing how a first meeting, no matter how protracted, almost never creates the same degree of informality as that generated by the interval between two short meetings.

The first to enter the room was Naima's mother: middle-aged, sallow-complexioned, tolerably good-looking—I thought. Next came Naima's sister. She looked more like a younger sister of the middle-aged lady, with nothing striking about her. The last to enter was Naima herself. She was truly stunning.

I had thought I would spend at most an hour with them. But I ended up spending the whole evening. By the time I got up to leave, I had become thoroughly acquainted with the entire family and their past life.

The hospitality started with fried snacks. Later, the older daughter, succumbing to the old lady's persistent requests, sang a Mira *bhajan* for me, and Naima, again at her mother's behest, played a cracked disk on the gramophone, to which I listened with feigned interest. I was also formally introduced to the photographs which hung from the wall. One of these—a picture in copper tones, taken most probably between 1930 and 1940 and printed on orthochromatic paper—belonged to the girls' father. Like the occupants of the house, I, too, had to pick up the picture and look at it in reverent silence for a while before replacing it back on the wall.

I promised to write to them and apologized that I must do so in English as I wasn't fully conversant with the Urdu script. Throughout the evening I had noticed how my Urdu had amused them. I also promised to have Faiq's mother write to them as well. However, when I got up to leave, I knew deep in my heart that I was neither happy nor satisfied with this meeting. I noticed that everything which might be even the least bit offensive to look at had been deftly removed from the scene. Soon upon entering the room I had spotted items of laundry left to dry on the clothesline in the balcony. But when I got up to greet the lady, my eyes fell accidentally on the clothesline and I was mildly surprised to find it bare. It was as though somebody had in the meantime crawled to the balcony unnoticed and pulled the laundry off the line without attracting attention.

After talking with Faiq I crossed another item off the check list.

The pictures had been sent out to print. I expected them back within a few days. I would then send Amand the pictures of his family as well as the baby overall with the zipper which I had promised him.

I had met Amand on a lake in West Pakistan where he worked as an oarsman. He had given me the most detailed information about this region. He had told me how the lake was once the land between two hills and how the waters of the neighboring river had been diverted to fill it. And, there, on the island that I saw, was the shrine of some venerable woman saint. Formerly people walked all the way to it for pious visitation but now, since only a few could afford to pay for the boat ride, most returned from the water front after making their votive offerings.

Amand's family had given me coarse reddish bread of rice flour to eat and a single fish to go with it which he had borrowed from a fellow oarsman and fried for me. Color pictures were not the only things I had promised Amand. I was going to send him an overall, too, for his baby who was spending the last trimester in its mother's womb. Bundled up in the overall, the baby would be freed from the danger of catching pneumonia from the lake's cold winds.

Most of Amand's children had suffered from acute bronchial pneumonia—I had guessed as much from the description he gave of their illnesses—but he and his family firmly believed their ailment to be the work of some evil spirit, which, in fact, as they thought, had even claimed a couple of Amand's children.

Even in their wildest dreams, Amand and his family couldn't have imagined such an overall, let alone owning a brand new one. This overall was going to be the expression of my gratitude to them for their hospitality and service.

The list began to shrink—slowly, gradually.

In time I crossed off Amand's name, too; as well as that of the old Catholic lady who taught school in India to whom I had mentioned having seen the first resting place of Saint Francis Xavier at Malacca—that rectangular pit from which his body was later exhumed and carried to Goa and reinterred there. "I'll do anything you want," the old woman had entreated me most respectfully, "if you could, perhaps, send me a picture of that pit."

And I had promised that indeed I most certainly would.

I did some stock-taking of myself after crossing out the old lady's name off the list. I had been back in London for a good fortnight now and had started work on my new book. My life had swung back to its normal rhythm, the one it had before I began my travels to the East:

reading newspapers, writing, other chores, study, visits to the library, afternoon strolls, then TV and sleep.

One day Cathy picked up the packet which had been lying on my table for the whole week and asked, "Aren't you going to mail it?"

I was in the other room, so I asked, "Mail what?"

"This packet, addressed to Miss Naima so-and-so, Karachi?"

I returned to my study and asked her, "Do you know what is in it?"

"Two hundred feet of Scotch magnetic tape . . . made of polyester, right?"

"Is that all?"

"Well, the tape is enclosed in a cardboard box which is wrapped in soft padding. You have had the housemaid wrap the whole thing in cloth and sew it up and then enclose it in this manila envelope."

"But the tape—what's on the tape?"

"Your message for the girl—isn't that rather obvious?" Cathy said, returning the packet on the table.

"No, I wish it were that simple. For then, I would have either mailed it myself or asked you to mail it for me."

"Your friend Faik's message, then," Cathy said, thinking hard, "or maybe Faik's mother's voice . . . for that *sallow-complexioned, good-looking, middle-aged woman?*"

After a while she asked jokingly, "Which of these two, the girl or her mother, is likely to be the central character in one of your future novels?"

I remained silent.

"Still hung up on mothers, eh?" Cathy continued. "When are you going to outgrow this fixation? Why not the young lady then . . ."

But I remained impassive. My expressionless face prompted her to probe, "Well, aren't you going to answer?"

"Cathy," I began, "every single day for the past week I have thought of mailing this packet but have put off doing so for one reason or another. You have no idea whose voice I have taped on it."

"Well, whose voice?"

I ignored her query and continued, "I have ben thinking all week long whether I should send the packet to Naima. I ask myself, now that I have got the tape and have gone through the trouble of having it neatly packed, why not take it to the post office, have it weighed, put the stamps on it and mail it? But then I think, suppose I later regretted it, nothing would stop the packet from reaching her. I am finding out, for the first time in my life it seems, that whatever you have committed to another ceases to be yours."

"What, for instance?"

"For instance the arrow committed to the wind, the dead body to the earth, and . . . "

"There you go again," Cathy interrupted. "It is the Eastern man inside you that makes you say all this."

I continued. "Cathy, I am unable to decide what to do with it. Once or twice I have even run my fingers over the wrapping to see if it has gathered dust and then laughed at the foolishness of my act. There is no dust here. How can there be any in cold countries? Perhaps I am driven to do so by my desire to find out how long it has been lying on my desk. You see, in the East, they judge the length of time passed over a thing by the amount of dust it has collected."

"Hold on, let me grab a pen and notebook," Cathy said in dead earnest. "I guess this must be part of the book you are writing now."

But I went on. "Then again, it is entirely possible that I am no longer quite so anxious to send it off to Naima. The book eats up most of my time. As I work on it, I become completely oblivious of Naima, her dead or living family members. Moreover, a busy writer, in search of new materials for his book, soon forgets the people he meets and photographs during the course of his travels, and the promises he makes to them. There comes a time when these people, uniquely individual and vibrant with life, are transformed into mere characters, and all the places he has visited become the stage on which all the different acts of the cosmic drama of life are enacted all at once."

"I can easily use this material for the *Foreword* of the book, you know," Cathy said. But I continued in a slow, halting voice, "It is quite possible that Naima and her family have by now become mere characters to me and this packet no more than a mere reminder of the time when I had just returned from my travels in the Pacific and the Indian Ocean, of a time when I had noted in my diary what I had to do or send to whom.

"You remember I had told you how at my request Naima's brother had come to take me to their house, don't you?"

"Yes, I do," Cathy said, putting aside the pen and the notebook on the table.

"Let me go over that scene once again. Then when you have heard the whole story, tell me whether or not I should send the packet on to her.

"Well, every single object in that living room disguised an over-whelming desire to be recognized, to be esteemed. That is why every-thing that failed to measure up to their standards, that seemed mean or odd, or otherwise betrayed poverty, had been spirited away from the scene. Naima's brother, who suffered from some chest ailment, told me that he worked for the railway. But he never did tell me what exactly his job was. Naima, too, was more than a little diffident about the nature of her own work at the drug company. And time and again the mother kept saying, 'You cannot even imagine what their father was and all the things he wanted to do for his children.' But when I asked, 'Well, what was he?', she answered, 'An *artist!*' She also told me that Naima was born after her husband's death. It was at this point that they removed that picture from the wall and showed it to me—the picture of a young man shot on orthochromatic plate, who couldn't have been more than thirty years old, I thought, when he left her widowed.

"My earlier excitement at meeting the attractive widow had begun to wane in that stuffy, lackluster atmosphere. I was looking at everything without enthusiasm or interest. I was told that it was Naima's older sister who had inherited all the artistic talent of the girls' father—perhaps because she was fortunate enough to have been raised by him—for she sang very well and was an accomplished vocalist, while Naima, well, let's just say she had been trained for a career job right from the start.

"I was at a loss. I had no idea what they took me for. Had my movie camera led them to believe that I could, perhaps, put the girls in films? The accolades they liberally showered upon the older girl forced me to ask her for a song. Not unexpectedly, she declined. Ultimately, giving into the persistent, urgent pleas of her mother and younger sister, she did however sing a *bhajan*, by Mira Bai, I was later told. I was now beginning to pity them. The girl, or woman if you will, simply couldn't carry the higher notes of the song.

"Next they bragged about their record collection. Some of the discs had been collected by the girls' father and some, after his premature death, by their mother. One by one they showed off every single disc. As I looked at them I couldn't help feeling they were light years away from the age of 33.3 and 45 rpm records. They were all old 78 rpm discs—bulky and awkward, which you played by changing the gramophone needles every so often. Their center labels—depicting the yellow

Gemini Twins, an elephant trunk, a lion, a horse—were a novelty to me and I wanted to buy a few of these relics and bring them along. I had seen them being sold, along with used books, in Sadar, the city's biggest shopping center. Their grooves were all but gone, some didn't even have any grooves left.

"Naima's brother sat silently on one side. Outside the window daylight had waned. The middle-aged woman handed me a record and said, 'Here, this is their father.' I looked at the record. It had a light blue label with the picture of a pair of spotted deer and the legend: Calcutta Recording Company; Music by: R. C. B.; Orchestra conducted by: P. K. The remainder was in Hindi. The record had a hairline crack running all the way from the center to the outer rim where it had been deftly mended by a piece of copper sheet and minuscule nails.

"I asked them to play the record for me and they were quick to oblige. The voice sounded vaguely familiar. I knew I had heard that song in England at the house of one buff or another of old Indian music, but try hard as I might I failed to recollect exactly where. Just then I heard the lady say, 'Watch, here he comes!' What came was a piece of flute music. Naima and her sister pointed simultaneously at the rotating disc and screamed, 'There he is!'

"The record kept playing, making a click each time the needle skidded off the crack. Once it even got stuck in a groove so that Naima had to quickly life the heavy playing head and advance it a couple of grooves. I was trying hard to avoid looking directly into their faces. The flute intermezzo was incorporated several times in the composition and each time it was played they listened to it in hushed reverence, while I wondered, what if the record broke one day . . . what would they hang on to, just what?

"On my way back to the hotel I realized with frightening clarity how terribly incomplete all my notes were. The most they could do was tell me the names of the kings who had built those temples at Anuradhapura and Kandy. Granted, the accounts of the monuments at Delhi and Agra were somewhat more detailed; for instance, it was possible to find out who had designed a particular building, who the architect was; but could they tell me, would I ever know anything about the man who had actually picked a particular stone or slab and carried it there, or about him whose dexterous hands had wrought such marvel or that stone?"

"Well, let me tell you what to do," Cathy said. "Just let this 200 feet of magnetic tape sit right where it is. I think I know what it is that you want to send to that family. But are you sure they can afford a tape-player to listen to it?"

"I can easily send them one," I said in a choking voice.

"And make them realize that all you noticed about them was their poverty? That besides that snatch of flute music, to which they clung so miserably, they owned absolutely nothing? Surely you don't want to insult them, do you?"

Cathy picked up the packet, played with it for a few seconds and put it back down. Then she said, "Just let it lie here. With it before your eyes as you write, the individuals you wish to talk about will not turn into mere characters."

After a brief silence I asked, "Care for a walk?"

"Sure, why not? To my place?"

Translated by Muhammad Umar Memon

Muhammad Umar Memon

The Dark Alley

MUHAMMAD UMAR MEMON

His sister-in-law served him the meal. In silence, he began swallowing the half-chewed and unchewed morsels hurriedly. He was afraid he might be delayed and the funeral procession might move on without him. His sister-in-law noticed his restlessness and remonstrated, "Eat properly. The food is not going out of fashion, is it?" Then, perhaps regretting her sharp tone, she said, "I mean, what is the big hurry? Do you have to go to a movie or something?"

But to answer her was no easy matter. His hurried gobbling of the food, which had prompted his sister-in-law's comment, did not disturb him at all. He did not really have time to worry about such matters. However, her affable mention of the "movie" had left him squirming. Is it possible, he thought, that the people, that all the people, can be so heartless? Momentous happenings take place right in front of their doors, and they don't even bother to find out about them? The next morsel dropped from his hand onto the plate, and he stood up. Noticing his mood, his sister-in-law decided to stay away from him. He dashed out of the house. During all this time his mind hadn't stopped thinking about the tragedy that had struck Maulvi Sahib. Maulvi Sahib and his family might have been observing the fast, and this had to happen to them today! His mind full of various anxieties, he kept on walking towards Maulvi Sahib's house with quick steps.

His whole being was immersed in a deep sorrow. A five-month-old baby. That was no age for her to die, was it?—he thought. Why do people have to die anyway? Do they never notice, as they disappear from life quietly and mysteriously, the void they produce in the lives of those they leave behind? Only last year, with the little money he had saved for the rainy day, Maulvi Sahib had bought a pretty little cradle for her in Karachi. What must he be feeling not at her death?

139

Head bowed, he kept on walking in the light of the electric poles along the roadside. In a moment, one by one, the events of the evening began etching themselves, in their unique pigmentation, on his mind. Each line became clear, each image vivid, and the whole picture came alive.

That evening, just a little before the time for ending the fast, he was returning home after teaching school. All of a sudden he saw Maulvi Muhammad Azhar Baqa coming from the opposite direction, riding his bicycle. Behind him, on the carrier of the bicycle, sat his ten-year-old son. He greeted Maulvi Sahib on approach. Maulvi Sahib alighted from his bicycle immediately, answered his greetings with a cheerful smile and said, "I came to the college to see you the day before yesterday, but I guess you were not around."

"Yes, I had a few things to do, so I went home a little early. Tell me, how are things generally?"

Maulvi Sahib's lips moved in an effort to say something, but, the very next moment, a strange hardness spread on his face. He smiled again and said, "All right, I suppose."

At that time he could not have surmised the reason for that change in Maulvi Sahib's expression; even then he had noticed that there was a slight tremor in Maulvi Sahib's voice, and that along with the smile on his lips, there was a dim shadow of despair on his face as if someone was slowly hammering his heart with a point as narrow as a spear's.

The end of the day's fast must be half an hour away, he guessed. He mustn't hold Maulvi Sahib any longer, for he may have to buy some foodstuff for the *iftar* and would need to return home soon. Even then he casually asked him—without really wanting to have his reply, "Where are you heading, Maulana?"

He couldn't help but smile at the apparent stupidity of his question. Why, he thought, Maulvi Sahib must have come back from the University late and then thought of making some arrangements for iftar. He has a large family with many children: he needs to think of them if not of himself. Clearly it was a silly question to ask.

"Oh, I was just going to buy a shroud . . ." Maulvi Sahib said, as casually as one tells an acquaintance during a short conversation by the roadside, Oh, I was just going shopping, or I was going to the movie . . .

"What?" he was visibly startled. As always, Maulvi Sahib hadn't let his sorrow surface; nevertheless his mind refused to dispute the accuracy of the news.

"But Maulana, please tell me what has happened," he could barely utter those words.

"It was the five-month-old girl; you must remember her! She was the one for whom we went to buy the cradle together."

"Yes, so?"

"She died a little while ago. It is better, I thought, if we get over the burial as soon as possible."

Then he suddenly remembered. That morning when he went to the University, he had also gone to pay a visit to the Maulana in the Department of Islamic Culture. There Mr. Banna had mentioned that Maulana Sahib's daughter had taken ill, and that he had taken the day off. Remembering that, he felt the sting of his own meaningless talk and comments, and sensed his callousness. His head kept bending down with the weight of guilt.

"You go on Maulana, I will join you in a little while."

"There is really no need for you to take the trouble."

"No, no. Of course, I have to . . . ," he couldn't say any more. They shook hands and went their separate ways.

What a man! If I hadn't asked, he would never have mentioned the incident . . . Walking down the road he experienced an involuntary surge of feeling in his heart for Maulvi Sahib. He had no name for that feeling, but it flowed like a river's current, embracing and gathering all, with affection, longing and love.

Maulvi Muhammad Azhar Baqa and he were about a quarter of a century apart in their ages. Maulvi Sahib was about forty-five and had fathered, including the deceased girl, six children. He himself was a twenty-two-year-old bachelor. This association between age and youth had taken root and blossomed on the campus of Karachi University, from where both of them had done their Masters in Arabic last year. During their student days they had understood each other's temperament perfectly. Maulvi Sahib had never accused him of atheism, nor did he ever try to make fun of Maulvi Sahib's religious way of life, a way of life verging on asceticism. Maulvi Sahib, soon after finishing his degree, had found a teaching position in the Department of Islamic Culture at the University in this city and had moved here. Two months ago, he too had come to this place upon being offered a job to teach

Islamic history and culture and Arabic language in a local college. Maulvi Sahib's personality had considerable charm for him, for, despite being a *mullah* at heart, Maulvi Sahib was a man of neat and refined tastes. People did turn to him for answers to religious questions, for his verdict on contentious religious issues as well as for votive offerings, but, unlike the other *maulvis* in the mosques, he never coveted easy money or free meals. He was never so taciturn in company as to drive his listeners to bang their heads on the wall, nor so talkative as to monopolize conversations. The charm of his personality lay in his having discovered a happy balance between these two extremes. His temperament exuded sympathy and understanding, qualities which endeared him to people and made him a friendly comforter of others in their time of need. How much and how often he himself had suffered from grief and want in his life, nobody really bothered to find out, and he, reticent as ever, never mentioned his deprivations to anybody, not desiring to rob others of their enjoyment of pleasurable moments of life. Without fretting or getting impatient or disheartened, he had gone on enduring his troubles. In their student days at the University—while Maulvi Sahib was also teaching in a college for the paltry sum of three hundred rupees a month—sometimes during their conversations, Maulvi Sahib would suddenly become quiet and absentminded, as if something had begun eating him up within. At the same time, he would make every possible effort to ensure that his conversation, manner and behaviour did not betray his particular concern. A couple of times he tried to force Maulvi Sahib to open up his heart, but he would either change the subject, or, if pressed hard, would simply say, "It is no serious matter. Actually I am in a much better shape than most of the maulvis in my clan."

And now he had been faced with another tragedy . . .

There weren't too many passersby on the street. His head bowed, he was walking fast. Suddenly he felt the urge to smoke. He was a smoker, and after a meal the need to smoke became more intense. He had a pack of cigarettes in his pocket, but since Maulvi Sahib's house was nearby, he desisted from smoking. The idea of walking into the midst of an assembly of somber faces holding a cigarette between his lips did not seem proper to him. Obviously, he was going there to offer his condolences, not to socialize.

Although he did belong to a family which had received a deep imprint of religious faith and training, he himself was not greatly interested in praying and fasting. This lack of interest was due to his conviction that one could lead one's life simply by one's native honesty and goodness. He was not against religion as such, but he was convinced that following it to the letter imparted a certain monotonous regularity to one's acts and killed their basic spirit. He felt particularly annoyed by one of the elders in his family who, despite his regular praying and his readiness to advise others to follow the right path—this done while running his fingers through his white beard—would not desist from casting lecherous glances at the ladies who happened to be walking by him. Also, the same gentleman had never restrained his son, a doctor, from accepting bribes. If one could do pretty well what one wanted while remaining a man of faith, then, perhaps, it was better to be altogether without faith.

"Where to, brother . . . ?"

He was startled. He was so absorbed in his thoughts that he hadn't noticed Mr. Hamid, his colleague in the Department of English, coming towards him.

"Oh, nowhere special," he said. He was not particularly delighted to see Mr. Hamid at that time.

"Oh, come on. You can tell me," Mr. Hamid insisted.

"Well, there has been a death in a friend's family," he was obliged to answer.

"Dear fellow, you could at least have put on a *kurta-pajama* for the occasion. It does not look right to visit a house of mourning in your suit."

"Well, so long," he said and moved on, thinking that clothes did not really matter.

The death in Maulvi Sahib's family kept him perturbed. To begin with, he felt sorry for Maulvi Sahib himself whose aging face would now be lined more deeply with grief. But he also thought about the little girl who had been snatched away from life so prematurely by death's eagle. Once again he thought of the immense grief the dying leave behind and of the gaping void in the lives of . . . As if it were an unending cycle: a man goes through the moments allotted him to live; while he is living, he agonizes over the deaths of those who have gone before him, and in dying he hands over the grief of his own death to others. These others entrust this grief to still others, and the cycle goes on.

He was hoping that Maulvi Sahib, because of his deep commitment to religion and his popularity, had made hundreds of acquaintances, even during his short stay here, so that when he got to Maulvi Sahib's house, he would run into a fair-sized crowd of visitors. It was a shock for him to see only four people there. Maulvi Sahib's house was small and stood right by the road side. Four chairs had been placed outside for those who came to offer condolences. One of the chairs was unoccupied. The three people sitting were busy talking among themselves. Their conversation ranged over various subjects. Occasionally someone would mention the subject of death and Maulvi Sahib as well. A fourth man stood aside, his hands on his hips. Maulvi Sahib himself was not present. After a little hesitation he sat down in the empty chair and humbly asked the man sitting next to him, "I have heard that Maulvi Sahib's youngest daughter has passed away."

"Yes, master," this fellow who wore a silk shirt over baggy trousers and seemed a local resident of the Sind province answered.

"They haven't left already, have they?" he ventured timidly although he felt he was belittling himself by posing that question. Even if they had, couldn't he have spent a few minutes in quiet meditation thinking about the departed?

The man to whom he had addressed the question remained silent, but the person sitting at the other end enthusiastically volunteered the answer, "The body is being given the ritual bath."

The gentleman who spoke wore a brilliantly white loose kurta and tight-legged Aligarh-cut trousers. On his head he had a thin folding cloth cap. He seemed to be in his late thirties or early forties. His face suggested that he had been through many ups and downs in his life. He blinked his beady, shiny, curious eyes anxiously, as though he had come to this place reluctantly or unwillingly. Left to himself, he might have refused to show up here.

There were very few passersby on the street at this hour. These were the days of Ramzan when the streets would begin to become vacant early in the evening. Sometimes a horse drawn carriage would go by or a rumbling bus. Across the street, on the corner, there was a small cabin which had been transformed by someone with sense for business into a restaurant. On one side of the cabin was a cigarette and *pan* stall, which had a radio playing. At that time the Binaca Geet Mala from Radio Ceylon was on, and a few teddy boys in their tight jeans were busy shaking their minuscule hips to the tune of the song. With every twist of the hip they would knock off the ash from their cigarettes in a manner which they seemed to believe would smite their viewers, and then would mechanically raise their heels in the air, as if every limb of their bodies was vibrating with an unknown, alien energy.

He saw all that—and all of it seemed very unreal to him. The people near him were busy talking. One of them, acting purely on impulse, got up, went to the cigarette stall, and came back with a pack of cigarettes and a number of crispy, sweet pans which he generously offered to the others, ignoring him deliberately. At any other time he might have wondered whether or not to take offence at such lack of attention, but at this moment he couldn't have appreciated the man's act more. He too had a pack of cigarettes in his pocket, but he was refraining from smoking because it was improper to indulge unconcernedly in one's petty habits in a place of mourning. It was good, he thought, that that man hadn't offered a pan or a cigarette. Having to open his lips to refuse the offer would have been a prodigious undertaking. They began smoking away, masticating and gossiping.

All of a sudden, the third man, who, like the rest of them, seemed a devout follower of religion, and who had casually thrown a cotton towel around his shoulders, shifted in his seat restlessly and spoke in agitation, as if he had been stung by a scorpion, "What time would you say it is?"

His manner clearly told that he was not really keen to know the time. His question hid his helplessness and annoyance at, and a warning about, the prospect of having to stay there longer than they had all planned.

"It is eight o'clock," the man with the cloth cap replied.

"Someone should take the message inside to Maulvi Sahib to hurry up. *Isha* prayer finishes at eight: then people line up for the *taravih* prayer. When will we have the prayer for the dead? Are we thinking of staying here until 2 a.m.?" the man with the towel inquired.

"All right, I'll carry the message," the man with the cloth cap said. "But I just remembered. It will be pitch dark in the graveyard. Someone should also arrange for the light."

At that the fourth man who had been standing still until then, and who was dressed like an apprentice, moved forward and said, "I know I've missed my prayers. Can you get Maulvi Sahib to move a little faster?

If I miss my taravih tonight, it is I who shall be answerable to God, not Maulvi Sahib. I'll go and get the gas lamp."

The fourth man's departure was followed by a little buzzing, and then complete silence. He heaved a long sigh of relief. He wanted that moment of silence to become permanent, to freeze until all the formalities of the burial were over.

But that moment did not freeze, not did it become everlasting. It was a transient moment which moved on to become part of the past.

His sense of peace was suddenly shattered, for the man with the cloth cap was asking him, "Where do you come from?"

"Here." He gave a casual and snappy answer to avoid any further exchange with the man. But some people rush fearlessly into your world of sorrowful thoughts and subvert it instantly.

"I mean, do you know Maulvi Sahib?"

"Yes—"

"Where do you live here?"

"Near the post office."

"In the red house?"

"No."

Feeling disappointed in him, the man became quiet, and as if to wash off the disgrace he had suffered, spoke to Saain, the native resident, "I say, did the lad bring you the copy of the Quran with Abdul Majid Daryabadi's commentary?"

"Yes, but you had also promised to send the *Sahih* of Bukhari."

The fourth man now arrived with the Petromax and was offended to see the people gossiping unconcernedly. "I'm sure I've missed the prayers," he snapped, "It is quarter after eight. If people get up to offer the taravih-prayer, when will the prayer for the dead . . ."

At that moment Maulvi Sahib emerged from the house carrying on his hands the body of his daughter. His heart began pounding furiously. He suddenly felt strangely powerless and insignificant. And he also remembered that he was not clean. He did not even have enough time before leaving his house that evening to pour a bucketful of water over himself. For a moment he thought, well, who is going to know or care whether or not he is clean, whether or not he had gone through his ablutions. But that thought made him feel utterly contemptible the very next moment. Had he fallen so low as to begin to deceive himself as well as the others? He had not come there to prove to Maulvi Sahib that the news of his daughter's death had brought mountains of suffering crashing down on his head. Nor was he there because religion demanded his presence there. If that were so, then he ought to have participated in the funerals of his uncle and his grandfather who, only last year, had passed away within a few days of each other. He had chosen to shock and humiliate his father by refusing to be persuaded to join in the funerals. His mother got tired of arguing the case with him: he could at least show up at the funerals for the sake of appearances. But he declared that he could not pretend to do things that he really did not want to do. He would either fully believe in religion and follow it, or not at all. He was fond of Maulvi Sahib; therefore, he had come here. That's all. So, now, his head bowed, he was walking behind them all. And all these inveterate chatterers who, a few minutes earlier, had been unable to contain their urge to smoke or chew pan, were now outdoing each other taking turns to carry the body on their hands in order to earn reward in this world and the next.

When they had covered a little distance, Maulvi Sahib, handing over the body to them, went ahead to the mosque to ask the people there to stay awhile to say a prayer for the dead before going on to their taravih-prayer.

When the procession reached the street corner, a bus suddenly passed them by. They all came to an abrupt halt. While they stood near the curb, it so happened that a horse tied to a carriage decided to answer the call of nature. The water he passed splashed on the ground and bespattered everyone's trouser-legs. Everyone looked slyly at the others: then, as if by a silent pact, they averted their eyes from each other. They had all become ritually unclean. Now no one could claim to be cleaner or purer than anyone else.

They walked to the door of the mosque and waited there. He thought the Muslims excelled at doing only one thing—building mosques. A small town, like the one he lived in, had at least two hundred of them. And these mosque-lovers would find the filthiest place in town to build the House of God on—putrid muck flowed in open sewers, and the stench was suffocating. A resolve mounted within him: he would not go to say the prayer for the dead, nor would he touch with his unclean hands the pure and innocent body of the girl.

"You people go in," the man with the cloth cap said.

"Come, place the body here on the handkerchief. How long will you go on holding it on your hands?" saying this the man with the towel took the big handkerchief which had wrapped the body and spread it on the ground next to an open gutter.

Until now he had acted like a passive observer of all the goings-on but now, unable to bear the insult to the body, he could not resist speaking, "Gentlemen, you could at least place the body over there, on the platform of this tailor's shop."

Everybody looked at him menacingly, as if saying, Oh what cheek! how the devil did you, an infidel in a foreign suit of clothes, dare direct our actions? He was so scared that he almost flinched. Watching him from the corners of their eyes, they walked towards the platform, where they put the Petromax down and laid the body near it.

"Go ahead, I'll watch it," the man with the cloth cap insisted. They went inside the mosque. The man with the cloth cap sat on his haunches near the camphored body, and he stood nearby.

"I say, how long are you going to stand there? Come, sit down. Take a little rest," that man asked him.

"No, I'm fine here," he answered politely, thinking that it was his moral obligation to answer. He believed in respecting the dead—and here was the body of a little girl whose soul—the innocent, dignified and chosen soul—had appeared from behind its blue abode in the seventh heaven and, having spent some moments on earth, having smiled her enigmatic smile a few times, had gone back behind the clouds to the world of purity and brilliance, a world without our strange relations and even stranger prejudices. It was to pay homage to her angelic body and her sanctified soul that he wanted to keep standing with his head on his chest.

"I say, how long can you stand like that? Have a seat," the man repeated.

I can go on standing my whole life, if need be, though you will never know the difference . . .

"Where are you from?" To while away the time the man started the conversation.

A shadow of unpleasantness crossed his face, and it hardened, but he answered, "Aligarh."

"Which Aligarh? There are two of them, and both are large districts." The man paraded his knowledge of geography.

"The one with the Muslim University."

"Do you know Maulvi Sahib?"

"Yes . . ."

"From where?"

"Karachi."

After the prayer for the dead, he, Maulvi Sahib and the other four people were left behind, the rest having returned to their taravih in the mosque. The funeral procession now began moving towards the grave-yard in the pale, sickly light of the Petromax and the milky white light of the municipality's lampposts. Staying behind everyone else, he too kept walking, earnestly contemplating the futility of life and Maulvi Sahib's grief.

"At what time did your daughter pass away, Maulana?" the fellow with the towel, taking the body from the hands of the man with the cloth cap, inquired.

Maulvi Sahib must have been going through an emotional tumult, and though he must have found the irrelevance of the question irksome, he replied, "At quarter to six."

Like a paltry weightless ball in the hands of a circus juggler the body of the little girl kept shifting hands until they reached the canal bank. They were walking hurriedly. The sound of their talk often fell heavily upon the concentrated quietness of the surroundings. He himself, and Maulvi Sahib were the only people who remained silent. When they reached the bridge, the man with the cloth cap assumed the duties of the guide: "Go down by the right side of the bridge," he said.

They all alighted onto a dusty path. His feet seemed to have sunk into a strangely damp sand.

"Good God! What a filthy area this is! And then this sand!" the third man, unable to conceal his irritation, said with a frown.

"Turn to the right now, all," the man with the cloth cap guided them again.

This was indeed an uncommon kind of sand. It felt moist although dust also rose when they pressed their feet on the ground. There was also a stench in the air compounded of the smell of old things, of pieces of chalk, of chemical substances, and of burning dung and paper. It was the kind of stench that gripped your throat and began suffocating you as soon as it entered your lungs. The path was crooked as well, carved with effort out of thick brush. Proximity to the canal had made the area so humid that when some of them rolled up the bottoms of their trousers to avoid the dust, their calves began to feel wet and to itch. The crickets' chirping was piercing the silence. It was dark and still all around. The light from the municipal lamps had stayed behind when they left the main road. The elongated swinging shadows cast by the light of the Petromax on the lonely pitch dark night seemed awesome and unearthly.

"I feel quite scared here," the man with the towel whispered in Saain's ears. After covering a distance of two furlongs the man with the cloth cap again told them to turn to the right. In front of them was a mosque where some people had gathered in the pale and dim light of a lantern to offer prayers. Walking by the side wall of the mosque, the procession descended into the graveyard.

They were walking down a slope now. The body of the young girl kept bouncing from one person to the other. They walked another couple of furlongs looking for a freshly-dug grave, but couldn't find it. Maulvi Sahib's face now showed signs of exhaustion and a strange helplessness.

"I think this graveyard has been filled up and further digging has been stopped. There is another graveyard on the other side of the canal, isn't there?" The man with the towel finally said, getting tired of the search.

Maulvi Sahib's face reflected worry, but the man with the cloth cap immediately contradicted the view expressed by the man with the towel, "This graveyard may have spread far on this side of the canal, it's quite likely. But how can there be another one across the canal?"

"All right then. Put the corpse down and let's look for the new grave. It has got to be here somewhere."

Corpse? How could anyone use the word *corpse* for the body of a flower—a newly bloomed flower, pure, sacred, and innocent? He felt as if he was suddenly caught within a furious storm whose howling, merciless winds were lifting a building off its base and smashing it into smithereens.

Saain hurriedly put down the body of the girl near his feet, as though he had just been waiting to hear those words of encouragement. Then, for a moment, he straightened his back and heaved a sigh of relief. He seemed to have thrown off his shoulders, after a long and hard day's labor, a heavy bundle of gathered wood rather than something as weightless as a flower. Maulvi Sahib looked on in grief. His own daughter's body must have seemed to him like that of an orphan child's, an unwanted, uncared-for burden, which the staff of the orphanage was in a big hurry to get rid of and rush on home. He had been watching Maulvi Sahib, intently, whose sorrow and despair did not escape him. At that moment the light of the Petromax moved on, and Maulvi Sahib's face was hidden in darkness. He could not have seen it, but he knew that despite his remarkable restraint and self-possession, a tear or two of Maulvi Sahib's must have trembled at the edge of his eyelids and fallen into the empty hollow of the sand below.

"We came to bury Saiyid Sahib a week or so ago. I clearly remember we passed by the grave-diggers' hut," the man with the towel said. "We should try to find that hut."

Forgetting about the grave, they now went looking for the hut.

Even after a long search they could find neither the grave nor the hut. Even Saain said that perhaps that graveyard was full. There had to be another one, for the young boy had told him that the grave was ready. If the boy wasn't lying, then where had the grave vanished?

But the man with the cloth cap thought otherwise and said he knew what he was talking about. After an hour of all this, Maulvi Sahib got up and walked to the mosque to get accurate information. He returned a little later to tell them in a gloomy voice, "I asked a person in the mosque. He says this graveyard has been filled up. We have to go to the newer one across the canal."

They walked back the way they had come. When they reached the bridge, the man with the cloth cap advised them to go down by the left side of the bridge this time, but Saain said, no, they had to go across the bridge. Maulvi Sahib quickly intervened in this argument and confirmed Saain's version, adding in a low voice, "The man in the mosque also said we had to cross the bridge."

They crossed the bridge to the other side of the canal. In the pitch dark they were walking in the small circle made by the light of the Petromax lamp. He was following them, head bowed, lost in contemplation. All that had happened or was happening had an element of wonder in it. It was bizarre, like an episode straight out of *Alf Laila*, or like the eerie and ethereal atmosphere of *Tilism-e Hoshruba*... With every succeeding moment his mind stretched a little, until he lost sight of what was around him. He seemed to be in a dense fog which had sheathed the whole universe. Everything had become estranged from its form and essence and had become incomprehensible. Then he felt as if he was existing in a void, all by himself. The entire universe had become empty. Everything on its surface, the oceans, the towering mountains, vegetation—every moving or static thing brought into being by nature or human toil—had been shrunk and had disappeared in the thick cover of the fog. But then someone had lit a torch whose light had suddenly cleared the center of this semi-dark fog. In that clearing he could see some human shapes carrying a dead body. Their feet, mercurial in their restlessness, moved on continually. None of these people knew where he was heading. They had lost their freedom, and their faces showed their vexation. They seemed keen to unload their burden but their eyes couldn't see, didn't recognize their destination. Or, perhaps, the one who had deprived these people of their freedom, had left them to flounder through darkness for the rest of their lives.

After an hour of going by trial and error they entered the graveyard area. The third man shivered to see all those graves around. They stopped in front of the grave-diggers' hut. The sound of their voices spread in the air; then there were some steady, repeated knocks on the door but no one emerged from the hut. A twelve- or thirteen-year-old boy standing nearby came forward and said, "Come, I'll show you the grave. The grave-diggers are my brothers. They have gone for their meal." When they were ready to follow him, the boy said mockingly, "Don't you want the stone slab?"

While they were trying to decide who should carry the slab, he came forward, lifted the slab and, as before, followed the rest. A little later they reached a newly-dug grave. The boy pointed towards it, "This is it."

They gathered around the grave forming a semi-circle.

"Say Allah's name and lower the body into the grave. Why wait any longer?" the man with the cloth cap said to Maulvi Sahib.

The grave was no wider than the span of one's hand. The man with the cloth cap found it necessary to comment on the situation, "What a narrow grave the miserable rascals have dug? And themselves, they have disappeared. Who the devil is going to put all the dirt back in?"

Separated from the rest of them, he stood and watched. The man with the towel lifted the Petromax, and Maulvi Sahib, undergoing God knows what deep, desolate and devastating states of feeling, lowered the body into the grave. As he did that, his hands shook slightly, like the hands of a helpless man who, facing bayonets, is forced to hand over all he has to the robbers. That moment was more delicate and sacred than the resounding silence, but its sanctity was defiled by the speech of the man with the towel, "Remember, her head should face Kaaba."

It was a moment of unimaginable misery for Maulvi Sahib; nonetheless, he replied, "Yes, that is how I've placed my little baby."

"Now undo both the belts, the one around the middle and the one at the feet," the fourth man said in a firm voice.

Maulvi Sahib did that and then parted the folds of the shroud to have a last look at her face. No one could say what the others went through, but he was simply shaken up. Such rosy and healthy cheeks! The eyelids drawn together like the petals of a bud about to blossom. A round, delicate, innocent face—even angels would have sworn by her sanctity. Looking at her, who could say she had passed away, she had just shut her eyes for a nap. Drip, drip. Two tears trickled down his cheeks and disappeared in the ground. Maulvi Sahib's condition was no different from his, but the faces of the rest of them were devoid of any feeling, flat and styptic, as if what they had witnessed was a routine occurrence, something quite quotidian, quite unworthy of being moved by.

Maulvi Sahib didn't even see her to his heart's content and had to cover her face.

"Here, Maulvi Sahib. Sprinkle some rose-water and the square tablets of camphor. Maulvi Sahib sprinkled a bit of perfume, put camphor in the grave, and taking the stone slab from his hands, covered the opening in the grave—sealing off a tragic chapter in the pallid book of life. Now nothing—neither devotion, nor regard for sanctity, nor prayers—will every be able to send a tremor of life through her again.

As soon as the slab was fitted, they assaulted that two-foot-long grave, hurriedly pushing the soil back in, so as to bring to a quick end the heavy monotony of the job.

He stood apart from the rest and looked on. He wanted to put a fistful of soil in and was also aware that the others were secretly observing his every move, and there was only hatred and contempt for him in their eyes, but the thought of his uncleanliness held him back.

The man with the cloth cap said, "Get those damned ones here,"— he meant the grave-diggers. "How can we put all this earth back in with our bare hands?"

"The scoundrels' hearts have turned into stone. See how they shirk work! But just watch how they will trip over each other to collect their payment," the man with the towel said. "Hey you," he looked at the young boy. "What do you think you are doing standing there? Go get a shovel and a jug of water."

"Sir, there is no water," the boy said and hurriedly brought a shovel. The four of them piled up the soil on the grave and leveled it with the shovel. All alone, Maulvi Sahib was being swept in the swift and fierce current of his grief. He too was feeling a wave of pain, deep enough to keep him distraught for the rest of his life, surge forth from his being. The man with the cloth cap called the young boy in his heavy voice, "Why don't you bring the water?"

"But, sir, there is no water here."

"Why not?" his tone was harsh.

The man with the cloth cap scolded the boy. Then they all raised their hands to pray for the soul of the departed. Quite intentionally he did not raise his hand but stood reverently motionless. He was not confident that the prayers really mattered. It seemed to him sheer mockery that he, sinful as he was, should be praying that the soul of someone as innocent as that little girl should receive God's mercy and blessing.

The man with the towel swiftly passed his hands over his face to end the prayer and said, "Let's get moving. Do we want to stay in this junkyard the whole night?" Maulvi Sahib could do nothing but look at the man in utter disbelief.

They all started walking; he followed them. When they reached the hut, the boy asked for the payment for the services.

The man with the cotton cap stopped, took out a lot of change from his side pocket, and paid the boy.

They all started walking again. The boy also came along.

Laughing, the man with the towel spoke frankly to the boy, "You thieving rascal, you didn't bring the water."

This gaiety seemed totally out of place.

"Sir, you know there's no water to be found around here. Tomorrow I'll bring some water from the well and sprinkle it on the grave," the boy replied.

"Why not from the canal?"

"All right, if you wish it," the boy was obliging.

"And what if the canal dries up by tomorrow?" the fourth man said in jest. Everyone, except him and Maulvi Sahib, laughed. The sound of their laughter burst into splinters in the mysterious stillness.

"All right, remember to sprinkle the water early tomorrow. We'll be back before seven."

"Yes, sir."

"Do we know the way back?" the man with the cloth cap inquired from the others.

"I can show you the way up to the bridge," the boy said.

"The hell you can. There's nothing you can show us that we do not know already?" the man with the towel retorted impatiently, as though he had been publicly humiliated. "I have been here so many times that I know the goddam way by heart now. I wouldn't be lying if I said that I come here at least twice a week. One earns merit by carrying the dead to their final resting places and by pouring dirt in their graves."

Now they started walking again, exchanging anecdotes and jests. They were like school children who had just been released from the solitary confinement of a three-hour exam and wanted to joke away their vexation. Some had even lit their cigarettes. He was still following them all. Suddenly Saain put his hand on the shoulder of the man with the towel and spoke confidentially, "Poor Maulvi Sahib! He must be overcome by grief!"

The man with the towel scoffed at this comment and whispered, "Oh, come come, Saain. Are you going nuts? The dead are soon forgotten. And how long can one go on lamenting the death of a girl the size of your hand? By tomorrow, all this will be as though it had happened centuries ago."

These words and phrases rustled in his ears. He felt as if molten lead was being poured in them, or as if a bullet had gone right through his heart.

They crossed the bridge and reached the other side. It was about half past eleven. The lights were flickering in the corner cigarette store. The radio was playing the song, "Someday when you are lonely, you'll remember me." A few teenagers were busy playing their noisy games. A drunken man leaning by the lamppost was repeating a line from a song: "Laila, my love, my love."

Saain said, "Wait. Let's have some pans."

They had their pans. Maulvi Sahib and he stood by, wondering at this disparity in people's behavior.

"Put out the light. It costs money, you know," the man with the towel ordered the fourth man, who immediately obeyed the command.

Now they were on the paved road walking in the light of the lamp posts, still joking with each other as if nothing at all had happened an hour ago, as if they had not been to the graveyard. Their faces showed a lack of concern and a contentedness one notices on the faces of the laborers coming out of the cinema hall after the late night show. One loving look at a lady's coquettish swing of the hip or some other blandishment had made them forget the distress of a hard day's toil, of perspiring and getting scorched in the sun.

At the next turning, he shook hands with the anxious and perturbed Maulvi Sahib and said goodbye to him. Then, leaving the brightly lit road, he entered a narrow unlit alley to go to his house. The alley was dark; yet, strangely enough, he could see his way through it clearly.

Translated by Faruq Hassan

Surender Parkash

Wood Chopped in the Jungle

SURENDER PARKASH

It happened thousands of years ago. There was a city called "That" on the bank of the river called "It," in which a person named "I" used to live.

When the news of "I's" crucifixion reached us we cast all the wood we had chopped in the jungle into the river, and the river itself was coming at the black ocean, hissing like some crazed snake.

"We're such unfortunate people!" our father said as he shook out the twigs and shavings caught in his white beard. "Now there will be hard times; there will be snow storms but we won't even have a bit of straw to build a fire with."

Our father's face was withered. His long white beard was getting blown around by the wind. We gripped our axes more firmly and started gathering around him. The tides were rising and falling in his eyes. He gazed at us steadily, trying to hold back his tears, lest our—his children's—hearts break.

Our sister asked, as she gathered up chunks of roasted meat in her sack, "How many times altogether are they going to crucify 'I'?"

"One more time!" our father gave a brief answer, and we heard the sound of a heavy stone rolling down into the river. "Come, let's lock the coffin which has just arrived in the graveyard."

And we dutifully followed our father.

The walls around the graveyard had not been built yet, and the command had not been given yet to shoot down the birds hopping in the grapevines with slingshots. They were all free—even the silkworms which fed on the leaves of the mulberry—men dug graves with their long fingernails and women swept the dirt from the ground with their long hair.

This is a graveyard—here the birthdate is placed on each coffin and

159

it is located methodically and according to its numerical order. Dust had gathered on all the coffins—all, that is, but the new one.

"Open it up and take a good look. Make sure it is empty, for it is 'I's' coffin." Our father's voice broke as he said the words.

Our brother came forward and put "I's" birth date on the wooden box and wrote on it, "This tomb is empty, because it belongs to 'I'," and then we covered it up with grape-leaves.

We came back once more to the bank of the river and sat down—the river into which we had cast the wood we had chopped with our own hands—and the river was advancing slowly towards the black ocean. Along the way was "That" city, where they sell watermelons halved like human heads. The heads of our friends dangle from the city gate with blood dripping from the severed necks in a steady trickle.

"Everything else will disappear. But blood stains can never be removed from stone," our father said as he washed his face in the river. The wet hairs of his moustache and beard were sticking together.

Our sister looked at his face anxiously and said in a sinking voice, "There are some marks on your face in spite of your washing."

Our father washed his face once more and kept it hidden in the palms of his hands until darkness had spread all around.

Everything had become black in the darkness—the sky, the water in the river, even the grass on the riverbanks.

Then, in an altered voice, our father explained to us: "You're going to tell us a story because you're the son, and then when you become a father, your sons will tell you stories. Times are different now. Stories are not about the past, but the present. Hang your feet down in the river and look at the twinkling stars!"

The surroundings had become full of mystery. Far away, in the grapevines spread over the new coffin, the birds huddled in their nests had gone to sleep. Some men on horseback entered the city gate and then the lamps went out. The blood oozing from the severed heads of our comrades fell on the stones and congealed into dark stains.

In the morning when we woke up, our father had already died. His face was still hidden in his palms.

His corpse was placed in "I's" empty coffin. Our brother then came forward and inscribed our father's date of birth and then these words: "His body has been placed in 'I's' coffin for that day when 'I' will be crucified a second time, so that he can witness the event himself and feel remorse to his heart's content." And then he burst into tears.

Our sister gathered up chunks of roasted meat and started wandering along the banks of the river in search of her children. And we turned toward the city in search of ours.

It had started snowing heavily in the jungle and our axes were buried in snow. And the sound of our sister's keening came from far away.

We are the wood chopped in the jungle! The wood!
The river is calling us! Calling us!
The merciless river!
Carries us to the sea! Carries us!
The merciless river!

It happened thousands of years ago. There was a city called "That" built on the bank of the river called "It" where "I" used to live.

The people of the city had cast everything they had into the river, until they had nothing left except their children and their grain. Their clothing was black and they had white cloth tied around their heads. And they all used to wander in marketplaces with their hands folded on their chests.

The night was creeping in slowly and the river advanced towards the dark ocean with a droning sound and everyone was watching to see how burdened the river's maw was from the accumulated weight of all their belongings. Then night moved in and the waters of the river became black.

On waking up the next morning no one even remembered what all it was that had been lost and how much hard work had gone into getting it. For the very last person who had jumped into the river with his hands upon his breast had said in a loud voice:

"Countless hands will rise up from the river and will deliver all the things safely on the banks."

"I" live in the city on the bank of the river "It." It so happened one day that "I" was feeling very despondent. I started to walk along the riverbank and ended up quite far away. A heavy wind was blowing from east to west. The trees and bushes seemed to be whispering among themselves. Several times it struck me that perhaps they were saying something about me—but then I thought, "How well are we acquainted, anyway?"

Reaching a certain spot, I felt that it was not possible to go any further, because the river had spread so much that no land could be seen on which to put one's foot. I stopped and looked all around. There was shoreless vastness all around. Suddenly splashes were heard from the river. I looked closely—a tiny boat was coming toward me from far away and the sound was that of rowing! I stopped in astonishment. When the boat came a little closer I realized that there was no one in it. And the oars were actually a pair of hands cutting through the water like a swimmer's.

In just a few minutes, the boat, which was a big old water-worn wooden chest, came right up to me and stopped. The water slithered under it and flowed on. And some hands from its bottom beckoned me to come towards them. I put my feet into the water, which wasn't too deep and reached the chest quite quickly.

In the still half-light that hung all around those hands seemed infinitely kind and reassuring to me. Soon they stretched towards me and opened up. I felt they were saying something. And for the first time I realized that things other than faces could produce impressions and that things other than tongues could also speak.

I don't know why I felt that they had spoken and that I had understood it all. Then those hands fell back down into the water and disappeared. The chest was bobbing up and down in front of me. I reached out and pulled the chest towards myself, and then shoving it gently, brought it to my house.

In the city on the riverbank where I live, the rumor spread quickly that I had found an old chest in the river, which was filled with some ancient treasure.

There was a huge padlock on the chest to which we didn't have a key; there was some writing on one of the top planks which we couldn't decipher. Thousands of people came every day to look at the chest and asked me where and how I had come upon it. I was obligated to relate the whole story of its finding over and over again.

Finally, the news reached the government. One day the officials came and took me into custody on the charge that I had failed to notify them about finding the treasure of my own accord. It was decided that the chest should be opened.

Some strong men brought large hammers and struck blows one after another against the padlock. After considerable trouble they managed to break open the lock.

Everyone opened the lid together and then the air resounded with screams, which included my own muffled screams. Out of terror, people began to bolt, until at last I was left alone there.

It was absolutely true. Whatever the others and I saw was no illusion—it was quite the right thing. It was my own corpse that lay in this coffin. And there were holes pierced in the head, hands and feet of the corpse.

It had been resolved that I should be crucified at the main square of the city-on-the-riverbank where I live, and that my corpse be placed in this very coffin which, after it has been inscribed with my date of birth, will be dumped into the river, so that if there is a need in the future, the people of that time can crucify me again according to their wishes.

Translated by Sagaree S. Korom

Muhammad Salimur Rahman

Siberia

MUHAMMAD SALIMUR RAHMAN

A rowdier gust of wind came along. The window flew open with a bang, and as it hit the wall a pane, perhaps a little loose already, shattered and fell tinkling to the floor. The damp wind charged through the room. Whole stacks of paper flew off the tables, fluttering about, and sparks and cinders from the braziers spiraled before one's eyes.

The squinting clerk, Munawwar Khan, sat right by the window. The wind sprayed his back with fine rain, and then began bringing large drops in. He got up in a huff, tripped on his chair, and almost fell, in his hurry to shut and bolt the window. But a pane was missing now, and there was no keeping out the wind.

"Who left the window unbolted?" Munawwar Khan asked, as though talking to himself.

Muazzam Ali answered in a husky voice. "Maybe this morning someone opened it for a minute or two and then shut it, but didn't bolt it. Maybe it was the sweeper."

"The wind is coming in," said Munawwar Khan, turning towards the window. He seldom looked directly at anyone when he spoke.

"Block it with a couple of bricks," said Muazzam Ali. "Or have Din Muhammad do it when he comes back." Four bricks had been lying around in the room for a long time. Perhaps someone, sometime, had brought them in to prop a table with. They had never been used; but once in that room there was no possibility of their ever leaving it again.

"Din Muhammad's off sleeping," said the burly Usman Akhtar, who was wearing his overcoat while he read a popular magazine. "The tea will be stone cold by the time he brings it."

The wind kept blowing into the room. Sharafuddin, feeling very cold, jumped up and, taking the bricks two at a time, stood them in front of the broken window-pane. "It's stopped raining," he said as he came back to his place.

With the draft stopped the men in the room felt a little more comfortable, but some went on warming their hands over the two coal braziers with such concentration that it seemed as though that was their whole purpose in being there.

It was a big room in a government office. Plaster had flaked off the ceiling and walls here and there, and water seeping in had stained the walls in filthy blotches. The green felt table-tops were full of snags, blue and red inkstains, and rings left by cups and glasses. The corners had been knocked off some of the tables, and where the felt covers were torn you could see where the knotted boards were loose. Some chairs had warped or missing arms, and the rattan weaving of their backs was broken. File folders were piled loose on every table. A rusty steel cabinet against one wall stood ajar, stuffed with files, files slipping out of the bottom drawer onto the floor. It was close to the end of the year, and the year-old calendar looked as though it has been dipped in gravy and hung up to dry. In a clean, well-lighted room, perhaps the clerks would not have looked so sickly and mournful.

"Everybody's down with colds at my house," said Muazzam Ali. "Both girls, the boy, my wife, my aunt. She's visiting from Sakkhar. Got here and got sick straight off. What an epidemic!"

"It's the same everywhere," Sharafuddin said. He had got the palms of his hands warm and was busy warming the backs. "Not a house in the city has been spared." As soon as he said this, it occurred to him that nobody was sick at his house. He became a little apprehensive. "Why did I have to say that?" he thought to himself.

Munawwar Khan said, "It says in the newspaper that these winds are blowing straight from Siberia."

"That's right," Muazzam Ali agreed. "There's something really strange about this weather. Night before last I was out on an errand, just for a short time, and it was as though the wind had got inside me and was gnawing . . ."

"Siberia!" said Usman Akhtar. "Once I read—Ah! The tea's come."

The gaunt Haidar Beg, putting aside his newspaper, said disagreeably, "What took you so long, Din Muhammad?" Haidar Beg's tone was always disagreeable; even when he made a compliment or asked a favor, the complaining note in his voice seemed to say, "Oh, this is terrible, I'm obliged to praise you, to beg you . . ."

"Sir, drink your tea," said Din Muhammad. "It's hot, no fear! What kept me is this—that fakir who always sat on the corner, the one with the beard—well, he's lying dead in the gutter. I just went to see."

"Very likely he died from the cold," said Muazzam Ali.

"Very likely! The police have been called in." Din Muhammad poured the tea into cups.

"It's so bitterly cold," said Munawwar Khan. "The newspaper said that in Bihar, or was it Bengal, a hundred people died of cold."

Haidar Beg spoke up as he sugared his tea. "I say, Usman, what the deuce are those Siberians made of? They think nothing of ice and snow, but if you and I were there we'd freeze to death in no time. I've heard they walk around in that weather in ordinary clothes!"

Usman Akhtar, having neatly flipped some floating tea-leaves out of the cup with his spoon, turned and looked at Haidar Beg for a moment. "My dear Haidar," he said, "the Siberians are accustomed to the cold from childhood. Therefore, they don't feel it as we would. As for their wearing ordinary clothes, that is incorrect. They must take precautions. It's no light matter to survive the cold of Siberia. Frost or snow or blizzard, work must go on; workers have to get to the job; common laborers even have to go on working outdoors."

"Quite right!" said Muazzam Ali, nodding. "A servant is a servant. After all. Hence the saying: The farmer's best, the tradesman next, the servant last!"

"There's one thing one must keep in mind," Usman Akhtar went on. "However far you travel, however tired you are, you must not lie down in the snow to rest, even for a minute. If you lie down you fall asleep at once, and the game's up."

"Correct. One should not go to sleep," said Mir Dad, who until then had sat silent.

"There's nothing you don't know," Haidar Beg said disagreeably.

"Well, let me tell you," said Mir Dad. "My grandfather used to go to Yarqand on business. He told us that on one such trip his party was caught in a sudden blizzard. They lost their way. They had no idea where they were. They wandered for a day—a night—they were exhausted, they gave up. He and two others just lay right down in the snow. And their eyes began to close. But there was another man with them who stayed on his feet, and he beat them with a whip, whipped the sleep out of them. Grandfather said that whipping saved his life. If he'd gone to sleep, he would have died, no doubt of it. As it was, he lost some fingers and toes from his right hand and foot—frostbite."

Sharafuddin, who was holding his cup of tea in his hands to get all the warmth of it, was inclined to think that if he had been in Mir Dad's grandfather's place, no amount of whipping would have kept him awake.

"Siberia is a penal colony," said Munawwar Khan. "The Russians send their criminals there."

"Usman! Is that correct?" Haidar Beg demanded. Haidar Beg liked to ask questions, and never believed anything he was told.

"Quite right. Siberia is a dangerous place," said Usman Akhtar, handing his empty teacup back to Din Muhammad. "Anyone can be sent there for punishment. Not just criminals. Just annoy the Government a little, and there you go for the rest of your life. Only when you're dead will they send you home."

"It's all rot," said Mir Dad. "Dangerous? If the Arabs or somebody offered money to people to go to Siberia, they'd be scrambling to get there."

"Those who go will regret it," said Usman Akhtar, firmly. Usman Akhtar was not inclined to retract statements.

At this point the boss sent for Muazzam Ali and Usman Akhtar, and the discussion remained inconclusive. The other clerks turned to their work. Few people ever came to this office, especially in weather like this.

Sharafuddin went and sat down at his typewriter. He had to type two or three official letters and a report written by the boss. He had already typed part of the report; now he could not decide whether he should go on with it or type the letters. His power of decision, never very strong, seemed to have failed him completely. He examined his fingernails, then took out his handkerchief on the pretext of blowing his nose. He slid his chair a little farther forward.

The typewriter faced him, serene and tranquil, undisturbed by his feelings, indifferent as the dead. He thought how strange it is that the living should so depend upon the dead. Then he told himself to stop thinking stupid things, and put a sheet of paper into the typewriter to type one of the letters.

Haidar Beg and Mir Dad were arguing bitterly whether a big political rally the day before had been a success or a failure.

Sharafuddin finished typing the letters, yawned, and looked around. Nobody was in the room but Munawwar Khan and Usman Akhtar. Startled, he said, "Where is everybody?"

Munawwar Khan answered without looking at him. "They went to have a look at the fakir's body. It's stopped raining."

The face of the fakir drifted before Sharafuddin's eyes. A dirty, matted beard, loose long hair, khaki shirt, no-color trousers torn off at the knee, saliva drooling from his lip, eyes starting from his head. Often he held a green branch, a tree-branch, in his hand. People said he had lost his mind in the riots of 1947. Sharafuddin didn't understand why people would go out of their way to see such a man dead; he had been upsetting enough to look at alive. The other clerks' behavior disturbed Sharafuddin and yet at the same time he felt vaguely that the death of the fakir had somehow released him, that a small chink of light had appeared in a suffocating gloom.

He got up and went out onto the veranda. The wind, still blowing hard, was unpleasantly cold. The green branches of trees, rainwashed, swayed in the wind. Every once in a while a leaf would break off and flutter away. The wet cleanliness of foliage made the road look all the dirtier. Turbid water stood on it in places, and where there was no puddle there was a thin surface of slippery mud. Heavy wheels of vehicles had churned the shoulders of the road into a tacky mush. Across the way was a heap of rubbish from which a dark, foul-smelling liquid oozed. Sharafuddin thought that he would have to walk home along such roads, and his heart sank. He looked at his trousers, already thickly spattered from cuff to knees. He remembered a story about a man who turned to stone, first up to the ankles, then to the knees, then to the waist, then altogether. He tried to put himself in the place of that man, but he couldn't get the feeling.

Four or five water buffaloes, coated with mud, came bellowing up one side of the road and went on. He saw his office mates coming up the other side, walking carefully, holding up their trousers-legs. They were talking loudly, but two or three auto-rickshaws passing drowned them out and half deafened Sharafuddin. When he could hear them, Haidar Beg was saying, "I don't agree! He was murdered. How can you be sure? Things are never simple!"

"All right," Muazzam Ali said. "But the poor fellow was crazy."

Haidar Beg waved his hands. "How do we know he was crazy? Maybe he was pretending to be crazy. Who knows? He might very well have been an Indian spy."

Arguing away, they went into the building.

They had managed, Sharafuddin thought, to turn this death, this utterly insignificant death unrelated to anything at all, into a mystery, which they would go on wrangling over for weeks.

Mir Dad came along behind the others. He saw Sharafuddin standing in the veranda, and stopped. Assuming that he too wanted to go look at the corpse, and intending to save him the trouble, Mir Dad told him, "The police have already taken the body away."

Sharafuddin was irritated at having attributed to him a desire that had not even entered his mind. He said nothing to Mir Dad, but inwardly fumed at people who turned everything into a joke, a cheap and bawdy street show of which they were the smug observers. If I got run over by a car, he thought, they'd come running to look at me, too, not out of sympathy but out of curiosity—to see what I looked like mashed flat, dead. And that would provide them the opportunity to repeat a few platitudes about the transience of human life, and they'd have something to talk about for two weeks, even three weeks. Every chance they got, they'd go over the gory details: who Sharafuddin was, what he was like, what sort of car hit him, whose fault it was, how long his body lay there, who went to notify his family. . . . And every time they repeated it all, their memory of him would be mutilated further until it was entirely destroyed.

He took one last look at the mud-spattered street. The fresh, washed, green leaves on the trees seemed as if they had put themselves beyond the pull of the gross, dense earth below.

Back in the office, he warmed his hands over the fire for a few minutes, and then, tuning out the conversation of the others, began to type up the report, slowly, with deliberation, so that there would not be many errors. Not long ago he had been roundly castigated for leaving too many typos in the final draft. At about one o'clock the boss left, and after that people began to slip away from the office one after another. The report was done. Sharafuddin put the cover on the typewriter and went over to the braziers, hoping they might still be giving off some heat. Usman Akhtar was giving Din Muhammad money to buy lunch, and it occurred to Sharafuddin that he, too, might sit down right here today and have his lunch at leisure. Generally he ate lunch on his way to the other office where he worked part-time, buying something from the snack vendor in the street and sitting on the ground or on a bench to eat it. But today the vendor's stand was sure to be in a sea of mud, with water dripping on it from the *shisham* tree above it—dripping right into the soup pot, probably. He grimaced at the thought. He fished some change out of his pocket, stopped Din Muhammad, and told him to bring him some lunch, too.

Usman Akhtar, sprawled in a chair with his feet on the corner of a table, was gazing out the window. The magazine he had been reading lay on the table. On the cover was a picture of a he-man in full armor, busy dragging off a half-naked woman.

Sharafuddin felt a need to talk. "Usman," he said, "do you consider Siberia to be genuinely dangerous?"

Usman Akhtar removed his gaze from the window, stared at Sharafuddin, and replied: "It depends on your status. For criminals and the poor and down-and-outers in the gulags, it is a dreadful place. The important people, officials, no doubt live the good life, just as they do everywhere. Brother, where aren't there dreadful places? After all, there are slave camps here, too, secret operations, run by crooks. Pity the poor soul who falls into their clutches! For him it's just as if he weren't in his own country, he might as well be in Siberia, or worse."

"Ve-ery cold. A moment of carelessness and your hand, feet, nose, ears are frostbitten. They drop off. Lose your way and you're done for. Get tired, lie down to rest, it's the end of you."

"One must not sleep," Sharafuddin muttered to himself.

"In the depths of winter the temperature falls to sixty below zero. Hit the ground with a pickaxe and it rings like iron striking iron. Bread must be cut with an axe."

"Cut bread with an axe?"

"Yes. Not just bread. Meat, too."

"I can't imagine how people can live there!"

"They're used to the cold, just as we're used to the heat."

"What a horrible place! Cutting bread with an axe!"

Din Muhammad came in bringing their lunch.

"Brother Sharafuddin," said Usman Akhtar as he righted his chair and sat up, "in my neighborhood there is a man who has spent three years being shuffled from office to office. The paper work for his pension is still incomplete. He has teen-age daughters, young sons, a wife, and an old mother at home. In times like this, with galloping inflation, trying to maintain decent, white-collar standards—these three years must have been terribly hard for them. I'm certain they have had to do without food quite often. You tell me if there's any difference for them between here and Siberia. A person sent off as a criminal at least has—"

Din Muhammad banged the aluminum cup down in front of him so hard that water splashed out onto the table. "Mr. Usman!" he said, deliberately interrupting, "Drink some water!"

They said no more for a while. The food tasted very good to Sharafuddin. Sitting in a chair and eating at a table improved the flavors. The room which had seemed so bleak to him now appeared more spacious and comfortable, perhaps because it was just about empty.

As he munched away, Sharafuddin remembered something else. "Mr. Usman," he said, "somebody was telling me that from now on it's going to get colder here every year."

"I believe that. The weather's changing everywhere in the world. I shouldn't wonder if in a few years it started snowing here, too." Usman Akhtar knew that Sharafuddin felt the cold a good deal, and wanted to put a scare into him.

"Here?" said Sharafuddin, and stopped eating.

Usman Akhtar smiled imperceptibly at his success. "Nothing new about that. Tens of thousands of years ago the weather here was the same as it is in Siberia. Scientists call that period the Ice Age. Some scientists feel that a new Ice Age is about to begin."

"Then how will we live? We're not used to snow! How will crops grow?"

"Who can tell? Many people will perish. Some will leave the country. The rest will have to stick it out. As for the crops—well, Russia seems to grow grain."

There was another pause. Sharafuddin had begun chewing again, but he was also chewing on this horrible idea, this prediction, which appeared equally immutable and improbable. The sound of water buffaloes running and bellowing, down in the street, made his mind do a sudden somersault. "Mr. Usman!" he said. "Don't the Hindu believe something along the line that after death a man gets born again as something else? There's a name for it, I think."

It was Usman Akhtar's turn to stop chewing for a moment. He hadn't expected this sort of a question from Sharafuddin, who he had long considered as a silent, simple sort who would walk a treadmill all his life without question or comprehension. He wondered why Sharafuddin had come up with this question now.

"You mean transmigration. A Hindu belief. We Muslims don't believe it. Their idea is that if a man does good deeds, he's reborn as a better man, and if he does evil, then he's reborn as an animal—dog, cat, monkey, what have you. What put that kind of stuff into your mind?"

"Oh, nothing, I just wondered," Sharafuddin answered, disquieted, and immediately added, "You see, there was a fellow on the bus who looked exactly like a toad. That rattled me."

"Some people do look like animals. To me the boss looks like a bear. The way he walks."

They both laughed, and Usman Akhtar said, "Din Muhammad, you might as well get us some tea, and then we'll call it a day."

The office of the firm where Sharafuddin worked afternoons was not far away. Even walking slowly you could get to it in a quarter hour. But when he set out, that short distance coiled before him like a clammy horror. A sharp wind still blew. Rain came in gusts. The streets were all mud and water, and every passing vehicle sent up a splash.

On the way Sharafuddin saw ten or fifteen men, their feet slipping in the mud, pushing a bus. The bus got started, lumbered a few yards, and stopped again. People who had run through the mire to board the bus, or were still trying to get to it, gave up and turned away muttering angrily.

A short way further an auto-rickshaw lay overturned, shards of glass strewn all over the street.

Sharafuddin had not gone a hundred yards when right beside him a horse pulling a cart slipped in the traces and fell. The immense mud-splash drenched Sharafuddin up to the face.

A truck loaded with bricks had got its front wheels stuck at the turn nearest his office. The water lay in the street like a vast sheet embroidered with every sort of filth.

Before Sharafuddin went into the office he looked himself over and wiped his head and face with his handkerchief. His shoes had a thick coat of mud. There was an unbroken two-inch border of mud around his trousers' cuffs, and the spots of mud on his clothes were too many to be counted. His trousers were entirely mud-colored, and his coat and sweater were specked and spattered. Looking at himself, Sharafuddin could have cried. He had only two respectable suits of clothes. He would have to put on clean clothes tomorrow, and if the weather remained as it was, they wouldn't last a day. His wife would wash this suit, but what good would it do? If the sun didn't come out, clothes wouldn't get dry.

When Sharafuddin finished his work and left the office, it was completely dark outside. Colorful neon signs, mercury street lamps, electric lights shone bright against the dark sky and reflected with multiple brilliance in the wet streets and sidewalks. Darkness and artificial light conspired to gloss over the ugliness. Sharafuddin saw this with pleasure; it was a sham, but pleasant all the same.

The wind blew in intermittent gusts. As he stood outside the office looking at the street, there came a violent gust, and to his left, a huge billboard advertising some brand of wool came crashing down. Terrified, Sharafuddin set off hot foot, and at this point the electricity went off on both sides of the street. In the pitch dark, he slipped and stumbled into a pot-hole. He stopped and tried to let his eyes adjust to darkness. In the lights of passing cars, the shadows of trees, lampposts, and people whirled dizzyingly about him.

Usually he walked home, but when he got to the bus-stand in the plaza a bus pulled in that didn't look too crowded, and taking it as a godsend Sharafuddin got on. To escape the pushing and shoving near the door, he moved to the rear, took a good hold on the overhead bar, and began to look over his fellow passengers.

To his right sat a boy holding a big notebook. The cover was a picture from a European magazine; it showed a snowy forest, and in the midst of the forest a narrow path on which stood a hunter dressed in heavy, shaggy furs, and his two hunting dogs. The scene was wonderfully clean and pure. Sharafuddin thought once again of Siberia; again he envisioned the snow, the bitter cold. He ached to walk in that snow, just for a moment, to feel the deadly touch of the cold, just for a moment. He felt that if he looked at the picture only a little harder he would find himself standing on that icy path. He heard the hounds barking faintly. The picture was drawing him, pulling him in.

"Siberia!" his own voice said. Somebody laughed.

He came back to reality to discover that he had answered the conductor's "Where to?" with "Siberia" and that the students and other passengers around him were looking at him and laughing. The conductor smirked scornfully.

"He's off to Siberia," someone said.

A boy said loudly, "Even in this weather a real Siberian can get sunstroke!" A lot of people laughed.

Humiliated, Sharafuddin paid his fare and mumbled, "The station." The conductor gave him his ticket and moved forward. After this, Sharafuddin had no courage to look at anybody. Consumed with embarrassment, he kept his head down and looked at his mud-caked shoes. He was amazed to see that the shoes of the man standing next to him were clean, even shiny. He very much wanted to see the face of the man who could keep himself clean from head to foot in this weather, but the weight of his shame kept his eyes downcast.

It was not far to the station. As Sharafuddin made his way off the bus, some students pressed behind him, and as he got off one of them called out, "All off for Siberia!"

Another observed, "Even here somebody's ripped off a manhole cover."

"Means we're almost home," said the first boy. "There's the restaurant of the Jullundur folks."

A third pushed forward: "Mister, teach me some Russian, how do you say 'I haven't eaten for two days, please help me, I'm starving to death!'"

Sharafuddin made to cross the street at once to get rid of the boys, but an army convoy was passing and he had to wait. The trucks were covered with khaki tarps, under which the faces of soldiers and highlights on the polished steel of Sten guns flashed by. Guns were hitched to the backs of jeeps. The vehicles were going slowly on the wet, slippery road.

Luckily the boys did not wait with him but went on down the street, and Sharafuddin was rid of them.

When he got to his own street it looked utterly desolate. Al its potholes were half-full or completely full of water. The wind blew continuously, rising now and then to hurricane force, screaming as if it meant to blow away the trees, the telephone poles, the tin roofs, the houses themselves.

He thrust his hands into his coat pockets, leaned into the wind, and splashed along without trying to avoid the puddles. The whole day had been a vast, sodden, frozen, filthy, meaningless torment. The weight of it made his bones ache and his mind go numb. Now he understood how people who had lost their way got tired and lay down by the roadside wanting only to sleep. He longed to lie down in front of some closed shop, lie there and let sleep drain all the weariness from his body and empty him, completely empty him of thought.

Feeling sparse, heavy rain on his head he walked faster. The bang of a window on an upper floor made him look up, and he almost cried out aloud—it was snow! A myriad tiny white flakes whirling down in the wind. . . . At the same moment he knew the illusion for what it was, somebody tossing a bit of shredded paper out the window.

He reached home at last. A small two-room flat on the second floor. He climbed the stairs slowly, came to the door, knocked. Inside, his wife's frightened voice said, "Who's there?"

"Me," Sharafuddin said, a bit peevishly.

He changed his clothes, and sat down to dinner. The potatoes were over-salted. He considered complaining, but then decided that such little things were of no consequence now."

"Have Munni and Nuri eaten yet?" He looked at his two daughters, who were sitting on the bed, half under the quilt, busy dressing their dolls.

"A long time ago," his wife replied. "It's been raining all day long. The wind blew so hard, I'm worn out."

Sharafuddin made some vague reply. He was reliving the incident on the bus, and feeling all the more miserable.

All at once he stopped eating, and sat listening. He got up and went over to the window.

"What is it?" his wife asked, puzzled.

Sharafuddin opened the window and leaned out. At once the wind cut in like a knife. The little girls ducked under the quilt. Sharafuddin shut the window, latched it, and came back to the table. "I keep getting queer ideas," he said. His wife sat quietly, looking from him to the window and back again.

When he had done eating he told his wife to make some tea, and lay down, pulling the quilt over himself. His wife brought two cups of tea and sat down by him. "It's been raining like this all day long."

"I know," said Sharafuddin. "I'm worried it might start snowing."

"Snowing?" His wife looked at him. "When has it ever snowed here? I've never heard even old people talk of it."

"All very well, but there are a lot of changes going on in the world.

The seasons are changing. Just today a man was saying that one of these years we may get Siberian weather here, snow and all the rest of it."

"Si—Si—what?"

"Siberia. A place in Russia. This wind comes from there. It gets so cold there that . . ." Sharafuddin stopped, seeking for a properly weighty image. " . . . That people freeze solid while they're asleep. Bread and meat get so hard they have to be cut with an axe. It snows for weeks on end. . . ."

Saying this, he remembered Usman Akhtar's saying that the ground got hard as iron. In that case, he asked himself, how do they bury their dead? Maybe Usman Akhtar knows. He decided to ask about it, next day at the office.

His wife sat quietly and listened. She did not believe all he said, but felt a twinge of apprehension. What if it actually did happen? She tried to picture it, but her imagination was not up to the task.

There was a clap of thunder. The windowpanes shook and the iron mesh embedded in the concrete of the roof gave a ringing sound.

"A hailstorm on the way," said Sharafuddin's wife. "I wonder if it'll be sunny tomorrow." She brooded for a while. "If it does start snowing, prices will go up again. How will we manage? These clothes won't keep cold out. Or the quilts. Or the shoes. How will we keep the rooms warm? Fuel's already so expensive. If the weather has to change, does it have to be in our lifetime? God knows it's hard enough already to make ends meet. What could we do?"

It was no longer raining but the thunder continued. Sharafuddin's gaze roamed across the wall to the calendar, now on its last sheet. The picture was amateurishly painted: a bunch of nomads riding she-camels among sand dunes. The colors were crude. He needed to get another calendar from somewhere, he thought, and made a mental note of it.

The power went out. The room was plunged in total darkness.

"Go to sleep," Sharafuddin told his wife. "Sleep all you can. Once the weather changes, you won't be able to. In Siberia, when it gets really cold, people don't sleep. They whip one another to stay awake."

He fell silent, and then he began to hear the silence. It was massive, as it had been during the nights of curfew. It was as silent as if the whole city were empty, all its people gone somewhere else, leaving him and his wife and his daughters alone.

The face of the fakir who had been found dead that morning rose once again before his eyes. Sharafuddin felt a wave of pity for him. He had been mad; his world had fallen apart during the riots. From that time until his death today, so many years, had he understood anything that happened to him or went on around him? But on reflection Sharafuddin wondered if he himself were much better off.

He heard slow, ponderous footsteps down in the street, like those of someone walking the rounds. He got up slowly and went to the window.

His wife whispered, "What is it?"

Sharafuddin opened the window a crack and peered into the night. He could see no one; it was too dark to see. As he gazed, a lightning flash illuminated the whole street for a second. It lay deserted. Water splashed in the flowing gutters; a few raindrops flashed in the light. Then it was dark again.

There was the sound of a car horn far across the city—a lonesome, ephemeral sound, crystal clear as if washed of all impurities, a wordless cry of farewell in the dead of the night. He closed the window, returned to the bed, and lay down.

"What was it?" asked his wife.

"Nothing," he said. He lay listening. Again he heard or felt heavy footsteps down in the street.

"The ideas you put into one's head!" his wife said.

Translated by Wayne Husted, Muhammad Umar Memon and
Ursula LeGuin

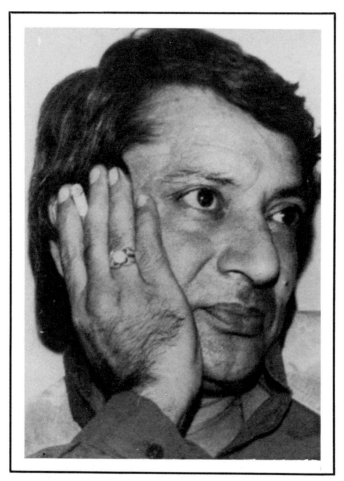

Enver Sajjad

Scorpion, Cave, Pattern

ENVER SAJJAD

If a scorpion is trapped in a ring of flames, it stings itself to death.
This statement has already been proven false.

In the corner a long table against the wall, with a piece of blank white paper lying on it. If the gaze is lowered along the right rear leg of that table, then on the floor, one foot from the table leg, is a covered drain that opens into the bathroom. Water from the bathroom does not enter the room through that drain. Sometimes, just sometimes, when the water flows rapidly, then right beneath the roof of the drain, where there is a hole, a drop gathers and runs down the walls of the small cave. Little by little like this, little by little, under the roof of the drain a small swamp has formed, it is like looking at a big swamp through the wrong end of a telescope. When the current of air moving along the floor strengthens for a moment, then from the trembling surface of that stagnant water a few mosquitoes fly up and sit on the wall of the drain.

The length of this tunnel between the bathroom and the room is eight inches.

If the gaze is lifted from the table in the corner against the wall, with a piece of blank white paper lying on it, to the wall, then on the wall's surface two fingers' width above the table is the sill of a closed window with half-broken, blind panes, on which an empty pineapple jar lies overturned in such a way that the sun's rays, despite being cut by the sharp lines of the half-broken blind panes, fall vertically on the jar.

Where the wall with the window in it rises and meets the ceiling is a rectangular pattern of light shaped like the window. The side of the pattern further from the window is three-fourths as long as the side nearer to the window. The rectangle of light, this half-transformed brightness of the intact portions of the window, is so perfect that even

181

the sharp lines of half-broken panes show in it. In this rectangle of light the inverted shadows of people passing outside fall from one direction, merge into the sharp lines of the half-broken panes and the rectangular lines of the window frame, and emerge in the other direction. On the ceiling the warp and woof of the motionless window, with its entering, merging, separating shadows, has been woven by rays refracted from the stagnant water outside.

In the background, sounds of the city.

In the air the merging, separating sounds of the city; the people entering the frame of light on the roof, merging separating; the jar lying overturned on the window sill; the piece of blank white paper on the table; the eight-inch-long tunnel one foot from the right rear table-leg, its surface rippling when the current of air moving along the floor increases; all this, all this mixed in together, blended in this union of vision, on which the present eye's curtain has fallen.

The curtain rises.

The air entering through the half-broken panes of the window, with the sounds of the city mixed into it, slides the piece of blank white paper off the table, the piece of white paper hangs halfway off the table, hesitates for a moment, is pulled entirely off the table by the weight of its hanging half, flutters, falls on the floor one and a half feet from the tunnel.

Now a scorpion's head emerges from the tunnel, pauses at the threshold of the tunnel and looks around for a moment, comes out. Its body is wet with the oily muddy water of the little swamp that has come into being in the bottom of the tunnel. On its back ride five small microscopic scorpions dyed with the same muddy water.

The female, bearing on her back the burden of five small children, advances. Three broken parallel lines are marked on the floor by her wet feet. Five inches from the pieces of blank white paper, a spasm runs through the female's body, the oiliness of the children's bodies slides on the oiliness of the female's body, the children slide off her back and fall to the floor. The female feels the burden on her back lightened, she turns and looks at the undulating, crawling children for a second. In this way her face turns toward the wall, with its closed window, its blind, half-broken panes, its shadows which enter the frame, separate, and are reflected on the ceiling. The female, after looking at the undulating, crawling children for a second, runs straight to the wall, and climbs it.

She heads for the window sill on which an empty pineapple jar lies overturned.

Five microscopic scorpions, because of their bodies' helpless trembling, slither along the floor very rapidly toward the piece of paper which lies spread out blank and white on the floor one and a half feet from the tunnel.

Now there is a tumult in the reflected moving shadows on the ceiling, and the waves of vibrating sound in the air.

In a dark corner enveloped in darkness, a male emerges from his hole. At first he lets his tail hang loosely, then he stiffens it, waves the sting like a rose-thorn at the end of his tail, grinds together the teeth of the plier-like claws at the ends of the arms which emerge on both sides from the point where head and body join; he advances. His gait is not normal. The juice and scent from the erect thorn in the prominent thorny surface beneath his stomach have made him feel intoxicated, the juice and scent which want to leave his control and enter the control of the female.

Looking around, he moves along with this gait.

Some distance away the female, enveloped in the same darkness, is absorbed in searching for worms, her gaze falls on the intoxicated male. To entice her, his behavior becomes even more intoxicated. The female becomes fully attentive to him. When the male comes near, she, intoxicated with his scent, allows him to touch her. The plier-like claws on the male's and female's arms clasp each other. Then the male begins to move backwards, it seems as though the female is pushing him.

Then another male appears out of the blue. The couple, clasping each other in their claws, keep moving in the same way. The second male makes a dash, clutches the female's tail in his claws, and a tug-of-war begins. At length the second male tires, gives up, and lets go. The first male, clasping the female in this way, continues his journey.

Then the foreheads touch each other, the mouths press each other, then moving over each other's faces like the touch of a breeze, they begin to pursue their pleasure. The female is not bored by all this activity, so the result of boredom, the female's tail lashing the male's head, does not occur.

Crowded close in scent and juice, this dance of utter intoxication continues.

Now they arrive in the shelter of a big stone in a dark corner enveloped in darkness. The male, collecting his remaining strength, pulls the female toward him. The prominent thorn in his juicy, scented, thorn-bearing surface, lodges in the female's juicy, scent-squirting hole, around both parts the erect teeth grip each other.

The male opens the plier-like claws on his arms and releases the female's claw. Once more he gathers all his strength and prepares to flee. But not enough strength can be gathered for him to free the teeth on his stomach from the teeth on the female's stomach, remove the thorn from the hole. He becomes helpless. The female's tail, like a whip, lashes the male. The sting like a rose-thorn lodges in his body, then she frees herself from the corpse, looks at it for a moment, then slowly advances and gradually takes his head in her mouth, begins to chew, begins to swallow. Eventually she eats his whole head. Leaving the rest of the body, she sets off at an extremely slow pace.

From dark corners enveloped in darkness a crowd of worms advances toward the headless male.

The female, moving at the same slow pace, arrives under a tub which has one side lifted up by a brick beneath it. Under the tub, reaching the shelter of the brick, she pauses, rests, continues to rest.

The magic of this event of the darkness becomes an ocean wave in her stomach and raises its head, flings her whole being against the hard surface. Then from the central hole in her stomach five microscopic children emerge one by one. After some time, when they begin to move around they come crawling and climb onto her back. With her plier-like claws the female helps them to mount, then without any special purpose she sets out toward the place where the eight-inch-long tunnel connects the bathroom to the adjoining room.

Arriving at the mouth of the tunnel, she slides off the edge into the swamp which has grown up in the bottom of the tunnel. After sinking into the stagnant water she comes to the surface, her feet, plier-like arms, and tail wave crazily in the air. She turns on the axis of her stomach, a typhoon arises in the swamp, tumult grows among the larvae, the mosquitoes fly up, the children quietly cower on her back, gripping her tail and quivering. In this state of going under and coming up, going under and coming up in confusion, her serrated claws happen to touch the edge of the floor. With immense difficulty she grasps the edge, plants her feet firmly, collects her body, and gradually reaches dry land. For a moment she stops at the threshold of the tunnel to look around, then comes out. Her body is wet with the oily muddy water of the pond, the bodies of the five microscopic scorpions on her back are dyed with the same oily muddy water.

Now the female, moving very swiftly along the window sill, suddenly pauses. Lifting her head, she looks around. Turning, she moves in the opposite direction from the jar, then pauses. She moves to the right, pauses, moves to the left, then turns and swiftly, involuntarily, runs and enters the overturned jar, in which the sun's rays, although cut by the sharp lines of the half-broken blind panes, fall vertically. The moment she enters the jar she becomes frightened and tries to get out, but on the high walls of the jar's round mouth her hands and feet can find no purchase.

Meanwhile those five microscopic children, slipping because of the helpless trembling of their bodies, fall to the floor and land at the edge of the piece of blank white paper.

In the jar, the female, trying to escape from the constant attack of the vertical rays, beats her head against the walls of the jar.

The five microscopic scorpions cross the border onto the piece of blank white paper, separate, and in the boiling madness of their veins begin dancing, begin jumping.

Then the tumult of the reflected moving shadows on the roof, and of the waves of vibrating sounds in the air, reaches a crescendo.

At this moment of crescendo the attacks of the vertical rays perforate the female's body. If a scorpion is imprisoned in a jar like this, then it dies from the sun's light and heat.

This statement has already been proven true.

Without regard to this truth, five microscopic scorpions dance, jump, one by one impress like a pattern on the piece of blank white paper the burden of the oily muddy color of the water on their bodies, feet, arms, claws, tails, and stingers, a pattern into which the poison in the stingers like rose-thorns at the ends of their tails has fully dissolved.

The dancing, boiling poison of the pattern on the piece of blank white paper; the lifeless body in the jar, a target for the sun's rays; the sounds of the city merging, separating in the air; the reflections entering the window-frame on the ceiling, merging, separating; all this, all this joined together, blended together in this unity of vision on which the present eye's curtain has fallen.

Now the curtain rises.

Translated by Frances W. Pritchett

Glossary

Abbu (*abbū*): a term of endearment for father (*abbā*).

Alf Laila (*Alf lailah wa laila*): *Arabian Nights* or *Thousand and One Nights*.

ana (*ānā*): a coin, the sixteenth part of a rupee.

baba (*bābā*): father; old man, sir; a term of endearment and respect.

barfi (*barfī*): a kind of sweetmeat made of sugar and milk.

Begum (*bēgam*): lady; mistress of the house; invariably used with *ṣāhib* or *ṣāhiba* to accentuate the sense of respect and formality.

Begum Sahiba: see Begum, above.

Bhai (*bhā'ī*): brother; often followed by the honorific suffix *jān*: dear.

Bhaijan: see Bhai, above.

bhajan: a type of devotional verse which uses *bhaktī* notions and imagery; earlier on it used to be composed in Brajbhāshā, but now also in Hindi; the name of Mira Bai, the famous woman saint-singer of North India who died in 1547, is closely associated with this poetic genre, which she used to express her ardent love for, and devotion to, Lord Krishna.

Bhatyali (*bhatyālī*): a popular Bengali folk-song.

Dada (*dādā*): a Bengali word for older brother; also used in addressing strangers or friends; it indicates a degree of respect midway between formality and informality.

dupatta (*dupaṭṭā*): a long, thin, gauze-like scarf, often startched and gathered in a bunch to form creases, worn by women across the bosom and draped backwards across the shoulders.

gulab-jaman (*gulāb-jāman*): coffee-brown fried dumplings served in cardamom flavored sugar syrup; a kind of sweetmeat.

Hakim Sahib (*hakīm*): a physician who practices traditional herbal medicine, as distinct from a *ḍāktar* (doctor), who practices modern western medicine; (*ṣāhib*): a title of respect similar to mister, sir.

187

iftar (*iftār*): the time when the Muslim fast is broken; immediately following the sunset.

imli (*imlī*): tamarind.

inqilab (*inqilāb*): a revolution; great upheaval.

isha (*'ishā'*): the last of the five daily ritual Muslim prayers performed a couple of hours after sundown.

ji (*jī*): an honorific suffix attached to names or titles.

Kaaba (*ka'ba*): the cubical structure in Mecca: Muslims are required to face in its direction while offering ritual prayers.

Khan (*khān*): master, owner; lord, prince; a title of Muslim nobles; usually added to Pathan or Afghan personal names.

kranti (*krāntī*): a revolution.

kurta (*kurtā*): a long, loose shirt.

laddu (*laḍḍū*): a round sweetmeat, comes in different varities.

Magh (*māgh*): name of the tenth Hindu month corresponding to January-February.

math (*maṭh*): a hut or monastery or college for Buddhist or Hindu ascetics and monks.

Maulana (*maulānā*): a Muslim individual well versed in religious law; a learned man.

maulvi (*maulavī*): same as Maulana, above.

Miyan (*miyāṅ*): an address of respect; sir.

mulla (*mullā*): same as Maulana, above.

neem (*nīm*): *Melica azadirachta*—a tree with small, bitter, berry-like fruit; its twigs are used as tooth-brush and leaves, in place of moth-balls to store woollen clothes.

pajama (*pajāmā*): trousers secured at the waist with a band; could be extremely loose or tight.

pan (*pān*): betel; a rolled leaf containing a chewing mixture of crushed betel nut, spices, cured lime and catechu pastes, and often tobacco.

paisa (*paisā*): a coin, a pice; formerly, the sixty-fourth, and now, the hundredth part of a rupee.

paratha (*parāṭhā*): a multi-layered flour pancake fried in clarified butter (*ghī*).

Pathan (*pathān*): name of a race inhabiting the hilly north-western part of the Indian subcontinent.

Phagun (*phāgun*): the eleventh month according to the Hindu calendar, corresponding to February-March.

Pir (*pīr*): a saint, a spiritual guide; a religious or holy man.

purva (*purvā*): the wind that blows from the east.

purvai (*purvā'ī*): same as *purva*, above

purvayya (*purvayyā*): same as *purva*, above.

raita (*rā'itā*): a kind of yoghurt sauce usually made of onions, thinly sliced cucumbers, green chilies, cilantro, and salt, or, alternatively, of roasted ground cumin, black or red pepper, and salt.

Ramzan (*ramazān*): the ninth month of the Muslim calendar during which fasting is mandatory on all capable individuals everyday from a little before dawn to sunset; Muslim fast prohibits all types of foods and drinks, smoke, and sexual contact.

Rigveda: the first and most important of the four religious books of the Hindus; consists chiefly of hymns in praise of the Hindu deities.

Sahib (*sāhib*): master, owner, lord; mister; a term of respect added to personal names.

Sahih (*sahīh*): name of one of the six canonical collections of the sayings and traditions of the Prophet Muhammad, compiled by Muhammad Ismail al-Bukhari (d. 870) from Bukhara in Central Asia.

Saain (*sā'īṁ*): mister, sir; a Sindhi term of respect in addressing people.

shisham (*shīsham*): a kind of tree.

shalvar (*shalvār*): women's trousers; relatively narrow at the bottoms but quite loose and baggy in the middle; worn with a long shirt (*kurtā* or *qamīs*); also worn by men in Pakistan.

taravih (*tarāvīh*): a supererogatory prayer performed only during the month of Ramazan shortly after the ritual *isha* prayer.

tākā: a coin; the Bengali word for rupee.

Tilism-e Hoshruba (*tilism-e hōshrubā*): "the enchantment which steals away one's senses"—name of a *romance d'aventure* in seven bulky volumes; a part of the larger *Tale* (*dāstān*) *of Amīr Hamza*.

vedas: the sacred scriptures of the Hindus.

Notes on Contributors

ZAMIRUDDIN AHMAD was born in Fatehgarh (India) in 1925. He studied at Aligarh Muslim University and later at St. Andrews College, Gorakhpur, and Allahabad University. He migrated to Pakistan in 1947. He worked as a journalist in India, Pakistan, the Middle East and the U.K. and also as a broadcaster for the B.B.C., Voice of America, Radio Pakistan and Pakistan Television. He started writing fiction in the early 1950s. Over the next fifteen years he produced more than two dozen short stories which show his deft touch for the craft of narrative fiction. Their provocative themes, the austere elegance of their language, left most readers intrigued and charmed. And then he vanished from the literary scene. Four years ago, after a silence of nearly two decades, he made a comeback, which was as stunning as his debut. A master of suggestion and understatement already in his earlier work, he stretched these qualities to the furthest limit in his most recent fiction. He wrote about forty short stories, a number of critical essays, radio plays, and TV serials. His latest critical work, *Khātir-e ma'sūm,* explores the dimensions of female sexuality across the entire range of Urdu poetic genres. A Hindi translation of some of his stories appeared under the title *Pahlī maut* (First Death) from Delhi in 1985. His first Urdu collection is in press. He was working on a novel before his death in late 1990 in London, where he had been living since 1971.

KHALIDA ASGHAR (now Khalida Husain), the second most significant contemporary woman writer after Qurratulain Hyder, was born in Lahore (Pakistan) in 1938. She started writing fiction in 1963, "to establish a contact with the mainsprings of my being," she says. After half a dozen brilliant short stories, of which "The Wagon" has become something of a modern classic, she dropped out of the Urdu literary world altogether. Married in 1965, she moved to Karachi in 1967. After a silence of a dozen years, she staged a comeback in 1977—wisened, more experienced, somewhat less willing to risk. The subconscious compulsions of a pained psyche, so powerfully captured in her earlier work, appear to have been muted somewhat in the stories of the second phase. She has published three volumes of short stories, some of which have been translated into Hindi. She is now settled in Islamabad where she teaches English in a girls' college. She participated, at the invitation of the Government of India, in a workshop of Afro-Asian writers at Delhi some years ago.

MASUD ASHAR is the pen-name of Masud Ahmad Khan who was born in 1931 in Rampur (India). He emigrated to Pakistan in 1952 and became a career journalist. After working for sundry Urdu newspapers, he finally joined, in 1958, the influential *Imrōz* (Today), with which his quarter-of-a-century long association suddenly ended when, in 1983, he was fired for supporting a petition demanding removal of the Martial Law and the restoration of democracy in Pakistan. With the change of government in 1988, he has now been reinstated. Besides two collections of short stories, he has also co-authored a book on the political parties of Pakistan and co-edited a selection of literary writing in Urdu.

SALEEM ASMI was born in Jhansi (India) in 1934. After migrating to Pakistan he took a Master's in English from Karachi University in 1955 and then decided to go into journalism, working in different editorial capacities in a number of English newspapers, among them: *The Pakistan Times, The Civil and Military Gazette, The Muslim,* and *The Times of Karachi.* He also worked as news editor for the *Khaleej Times* (Dubai) from 1981 to his return to Pakistan in 1988, when he joined the staff of *Dawn,* a Karachi-based English language newspaper. In 1969 he briefly worked as a Public Relations Officer for Pakistan International Airlines. He was also a member of the Pakistan Film Censors Board and of the Selection and Purchase Committee of the National Art Gallery. He is not a prolific writer. Nevertheless the small corpus of his writing, which reveals a mind steeped in modernism, has been generally regarded as pioneering and influential, and his translations from Paul Valéry, Camus, Jean-Paul Sartre, Soderberg, and Eric Newman have also been noted with appreciation.

(RAJA) FARUQ HASSAN is an Urdu poet who was born in 1939 at Lyallpur (now, Faisalabad, Pakistan). He holds degrees in English studies from the Universities of Punjab, Leeds, and New Brunswick and has also taught in Pakistan and Canada, where he permanently settled in 1968. Since 1972 he has been teaching at Dawson College, Montreal. He has published two volumes of poetry and numerous translations of Urdu poets and prose writers and has also co-edited *Versions of Truth, Urdu Short Stories from Pakistan.* A selection of his poems in English translation will be shortly published in Canada.

INTIZAR HUSAIN was born in Dibai (India) some time in the 1920's and was educated in Meerut and, after migrating to Pakistan in 1947, in Lahore. Creative writer, critic, translator, he has published five volumes of short stories, three novels, a novella, and a volume of critical essays. The *Journal of South Asian Literature* devoted an entire issue to him in 1983, and a selected translation of his short fiction works appeared under the title *An Unwritten Epic and Other Stories* in 1987. He makes his home in Lahore where in 1988 he resigned from his job as a columnist with the daily Urdu newspaper *Mashriq* (The East).

ABDULLAH HUSSEIN is the pen-name of Muhammad Khan who was born in 1931 in Rawalpindi (Pakistan) and now makes his home in London, where he moved in the 1960s with his wife. He gave up a lucrative career in chemical engineering—for which he was trained in Pakistan and Canada and which he had practiced for more than a dozen years in Pakistan and the U.K.—to devote all his time to writing. His short stories and novels have received wide critical acclaim in India and Pakistan; his first novel *Udās naslēn* (Sad Generations; 1963) won him Pakistan's highest literary prize, the Adamjee Award, and has been translated into Bengali, Chinese, Hindi and Panjabi. A Chinese translation of his second novel *Bāgh* (The Tiger) is underway. All except one of his short stories, of which he has published two volumes, are available in English translation under the titles *Night* and *Downfall by Degrees.* He has also written a novel in English, *The Immigrants.*

WAYNE R. HUSTED holds a Master's degree in South Asian Studies from the University of Wisconsin, Madison, where he is now finishing a doctorate on the place and role of the martyred medieval Indian religious figure Nurullah Shustari in Shiite piety. He spent an undergraduate year in Agra (India) to study Hindi and Urdu, and a graduate year in Lahore (Pakistan) to study advanced Urdu under the Berkeley Urdu Language Program. He has co-translated numerous contemporary Urdu writers.

SAGAREE S(ENGUPTA) KOROM was born in Gujarat (India) in 1958. She has lived in the United States since childhood, and has traveled to Iran, Latin America, India and Pakistan. She took an M.A. in South Asian Studies from the University of Wisconsin, Madison, and is now a Ph.D. student at the University of Pennsylvania where she also teaches Bengali. Her doctoral project will focus on the Brajbhasa poetry of "Bharatendu" Hariscandra. Her main areas of interest are medieval North Indian poetry and modern Urdu, Hindi, and Bengali literature.

URSULA K. LEGUIN is the noted American fantasy and science-fiction writer and poet. Author of more than two dozen books and recipient of many prizes, including the Nebula, Hugo, Kafka, and National Book Award, she has also taught at several universities in the United States and Europe. She grew up in California and now lives in Oregon.

IQBAL MAJEED was born in 1932 at Moradabad (India). After an M.A. in Political Science, he taught college for a few years before moving to All India Radio, Bhopal, as Producer of Urdu Programs. In 1962, he was transferred to Lucknow in the same capacity. He started his literary career in 1955. In 1982, his second collection of short stories received a cash award by the Urdu Academy, U.P. Some of his stories have been translated into Hindi, Marathi, English, and one also into Russian. His other writing includes about fifty radio and stage plays. He is currently putting together his third collection of stories.

HASAN MANZAR is the pen-name of Syed Manzar Hasan who was born in 1934 at Hapur and raised at Gorakhpur (India) before migrating to Pakistan in 1947. After finishing his medical studies in Lahore, he joined the Dutch Merchant navy as a surgeon and subsequently worked in different medical capacities in Saudi Arabia, Nigeria and Lagos. He later decided to study psychology at Edinburgh University. After taking additional degrees from the Royal Colleges of Surgeons, Edinburgh, and Royal Colleges of Physicians, Glasgow, he took up a teaching position at Malaya University, Kuala Lumpur. He is now settled in Hyderabad (Pakistan), where he runs a private psychiatric clinic. He has so far published two collections of short stories; a third one is in press; currently he is working on a fourth collection and a novel.

MUHAMMAD UMAR MEMON was born in 1939 at Aligarh (India) and migrated to Pakistan in 1954. He was educated at Karachi University, and later, in the United States, where he took a Master's in Near Eastern Languages and Literatures from Harvard and a Ph.D. in Islamic Studies from UCLA. He is now Professor of Urdu, Persian, and Islam at the University of Wisconsin, Madison. He writes fiction and criticism in Urdu and English and has also translated widely from modern Urdu fiction, of which four volumes have appeared to date. *Tāṅk galī* (The Dark Alley), his first collection of short stories, appeared in 1989. He has edited *Studies in the Urdu Ghazal and Prose Fiction*; and a book of his on religious polemics, *Ibn Taimīya's Struggle Against Popular Religion*, appeared from The Hague and Paris in 1976.

C.M. NAIM hails from Barabanki (India). He was educated in India and the United States and has been teaching Urdu humanities at the University of Chicago for a quarter of a century now. He has written several major articles on Urdu poetry and prose fiction and has also translated numerous modern Urdu poets and short story writers. A co-founder and a former editor of the *Journal of South Asian Literature*, he now edits and publishes the *Annual of Urdu Studies* and has recently published a book, *Iqbal, Jinnah, and Pakistan: The Vision and the Reality*, which he edited. Currently he is working on an annotated translation of *Zikr-e Mīr*—the Persian autobiography of Mir, one of Urdu's foremost poets.

SURENDER PARKASH is the pen-name of Surendra Kumar Oberoi, who was born in 1930 in Lyallpur (now in Pakistan). He studied Urdu from his father, a proprietor of a small store. He could not finish high school as India was partitioned and the family was obliged to emigrate to Delhi. A chance meeting with the Urdu poet Tajwar Samri inspired him to become a writer. After working as a scriptwriter at All India Radio, Delhi, he moved to Bombay in 1971 to write for the movie industry. Some of the movies he has worked for are: *Vijay, Apnā Jahāṅ,* and *Anāmikā.* He has published three collections of short stories, a fourth one is underway, and he is currently working on a novel entitled *Fassaan.*

FRANCES W. PRITCHETT is Assistant Professor of Modern Indic Languages at Columbia University and teaches Urdu and Hindi. Her research interests include classical Urdu lyric poetry (*ghazal*) and romance (*dāstān*), as well as modern popular narrative literature in Hindi and Urdu. Her Ph.D. dissertation on the *qiṣṣa* genre has now appeared as a book: *Marvelous Encounters: Folk Romance in Urdu and Hindi.* She has also compiled *Urdu Literature: A Bibliography of English Language Sources* and, with Kh. Khaliq, *Urdu Meter: A Practical Handbook.*

JAVAID QAZI was born in Pakistan in 1947 and came to the United States in 1968 to work towards a Ph.D. in English literature. Specializing in renaissance drama, he completed his doctorate in 1978 at Arizona State University. His fiction has appeared in *Kansas Quarterly, Sequoia, Chelsea* and the *Toronto South Asian Review.* He has written a novel, *The Remingtons of India,* based on the British Raj and is currently working on another novel *Alien Harvest.* His "Anaïs Nin's Louveciennes" will shortly appear in *Anaïs Nin: An International Journal.* He now lives in San Jose, California and teaches writing at San Jose State University.

MUHAMMAD SALIMUR RAHMAN, who was born in India in 1934, is an eminent Urdu poet and critic. He started his literary career with the translation into Urdu of Homer's *Odyssey.* He has worked as editor of the best modern Urdu literary journal *Saverā* and as associate editor of *Nuṣrat,* a weekly. Since 1963 he has been contributing book reviews and literary columns to the English daily, *The Pakistan Times.* He has published a great deal of poetry, seven short stories, and numerous translations from English into Urdu and from Urdu into English; three of his English poems once appeared in *Poetry North West.* Since the early 1980s he has been working single-handedly on compiling a comprehensive Urdu-English dictionary.

GORDON (CHARLES) ROADARMEL was born in 1932 in India of missionary parents and was educated in that country and the United States. After several degrees in English and a year at the Chicago Theological Seminary, where he was training for a career in the ministry, he finally decided to pursue his true love: Hindi language and literature. He received a Ph.D. from the University of California, Berkeley, in 1969 and was appointed Assistant Professor there the same year. At the time of his premature death in 1972, he had already emerged as the single most astute and sensitive scholar-critic of modern Hindi literature. Besides numerous highly acclaimed articles, he is also known for his brilliant translations from contemporary Hindi fiction, among them the novels *The Gift of a Cow* by Premchand and *To Each His Stranger* by Agyeya. *A Death in Delhi: Modern Hindi Short Stories,* which he edited and translated, appeared posthumously.

ENVER SAJJAD was born in 1936 in Lahore. After writing fiction in the traditional vein for a number of years, he opted for a more daring and innovative approach in the 1960s, producing a series of short stories which both dazzled and shocked the readership with their strident avant-gardism. At the forefront of the modernist movement today, he is also its most controversial figure. He is well known also as a painter, writer of radio and TV plays and actor. He studied medicine in Lahore and Liverpool (U.K.) and is a physician by profession. His active involvement in politics during the Bhutto years earned him the enduring displeasure of the government of General Zia-ul-Haq: he was twice imprisoned in 1977 and 1978 and was banned from state-owned radio and TV. He founded Pakistan Artists Equity in 1972 and later worked as its President. His honorary appointments include: Chairman, The Pakistan Arts Council, Lahore, and Member, Board of Governors, Pakistan National Council of the Arts. He was also a member of a three-man delegation to the Berlin Festival of Performing Arts, held in 1973 in the German Democratic Republic. His published works include four volumes of short stories, three novels, five collections of TV plays, and a book of critical essays. Currently he is Chief Editor of *Media,* a show-business magazine.